"Art of Self-Healing through Ayurveda."

By Vaidya. ArunaPatki
(Doctor of Ayurvedic Medicine, India)
BAMS, YOGA, HEALER, Integrative THERAPIST

What Nature says?

♦ **Our body requires 12 hours of rest for cleaning, repairing and to regaining energy.**

♦ **Our body is designed taking food twice a day depending upon a digestion and prakruti of the individual.**

We should give sufficient time for our vital organs
to take care of them.

Take charge of your life's energy.
(It is important not to work
so hard to reach the second wind.)

Preface

Namaste To All My Readers For Giving Me This Wonderful Opportunity To Learn And Practice Ayurveda, Yoga, Breathing Techniques, Chants, Mudras(Hand Gestures), Prayers(Gratitude), Asanas(Body Postures), Chakra (Energy Centers) Etc., through this Book. Hope We All Grow From This Science. Science Is the Structure Of Ayurveda And The Art Is How We Practice This Form Of Healing Approach On The Day To Day Basis.

Review For Dr. ArunaPatki

"Vaidya Aruna Patki has shared her decades of Ayurvedic Experience and practical tips to empower people to simply change their life with a mindful awareness towards health & well-being. This book contains may pearls of wisdom from Yoga, Ayurveda & allied Vedic Sciences. This book is just not about information but about real knowledge that become a part of your daily living."

Dr.Suhas K shirsagar BAMS, MD(Ayurveda)
Best Selling Author, Motivational Speaker & Medical Astrologer. Author: The Hot Belly Diet, Change Your Schedule,

Dipal Shah
Author, Energy Medicine Practioner, and Speaker
Ananda 4 Life, LLC
Ananda4life.com

When chronic or acute health challenges come along you are up against the pharmaceutical company and the doctors. Your mind doesn't function the same. You feel stuck and disconnected from the world. I felt that way for a while and had no idea what to do until I met Aruna Patki, a profound healer and teacher.

"Early 2016, I was facing a few health challenges that were keeping me confined in the house. I assumed if I eat right, they will go away. My health got worse. I started other routes of healing such as acupuncture, homeopathy, and western medicine but nothing was changing. It was becoming a greater challenge trying to find the right combination of therapies. I spend thousands of dollars over 3 years. Finding it to be the worse roller coaster ever. I was getting more and more hopeless and sad within me, even though I never showed it on the outside. I was strong and tried not to care about what others thought but I did care.

One thing I had never really took into consideration was Ayurveda, a 5000 year old ancient Indian healing practice that heals the body inside and out. Because I knew it was an intense process and I would have to change things.

I was looking for easy way out, like most people. The biggest thing I didn't want to change was my eating habits. I wanted to continue to eat pizza, chicken, pasta and chocolate. That was my biggest challenge. Until I ended up with a Kidney stone early 2019 and the doctor wanted to perform an invasive procedure. This is when I got my act together.

Something inside me was guiding me towards Ayurveda without a doubt. The moment I was told by the doctor that they will have to go break this stone up I sought out an ayurvedic practitioner in my area. I was determined not to confine myself to western medicine. That is how I met this wonderful, caring and kind human being, ArunaPatki, who truly cared about others well-being and scheduled me the next day.

I started a 10 day Detox, eating the foods and doing yoga poses that Aryna recommended. She explained how ayurveda works with the body with just simple changes. Throughout the entire 10 days and even now she is always there for me through all the challenges. She taught me self care which I thought I had been doing. I had been preaching self care in my own practice but this truly opened up another dimension of healing for me. I discovered how much I loved cooking for myself and taking 30 minutes to an hour of me time benefited my nervous system and my emotions.

I never realized how intricate and deep Ayurveda is until I went through the process. I have decided to dedicate my body and health to an ayurvedic lifestyle and have been enjoying it very much. Now I am on the right path the path to healing my body. I finally found the right combination of food, yoga, meditation, energy healing, positive words and a teacher. Healing isn't just about using 1 tool. It is a combination of tools that are always available to us. We just have to be open to them.

Aruna is brilliant. Her dedication to the human body, mind and soul brings clarity within each person and a level of enlightenment within. Going through the 10 days of healing was is a beautiful journey and I would recommend it to anyone who is tired of feeling stuck, tired of taking pills, and wanting to find a cure. Ayurveda is the way to heal the body. We can't only incorporate allopathy, we need to search and be aware of what else is available and what else can I do for me. This is very important whether or not you are dealing with a health issue.

Ayurveda is the best thing I discovered. It changed my life because I had the right person guiding me. My sincere gratitude goes to you ArunaPatki for showing me the path to greater well-being. Thank you. You are the best and may you be blessed with sharing your knowledge with the world."

Jai Dhanwantari, Vaidya Gaurang Joshi,
International Ayurveda Physician,
Director- Atharva Multi-Specialty Ayurveda
Hospital and Research Center,
Rajkot,Gujarat,India.

Dear Readers,
It's really a great pleasure to write a foreward o this book name "Art of Self-Healing through Ayurveda"written by Vaidya Aruna Patki, from Charlotte, NC, USA, Iknow Vd.Aruna since along and she is spreading the science of life Ayurveda in the west with her great efforts and dedicatedly and as I said Ayurveda is the science of life she has covered almost all aspects of Ayurveda in this book.

Starting from aims and objectives of Ayurveda she has emphasized on Diet that is very important part of Ayurveda as Ayurveda strongly believes your food is your medicine so by eating appropriate food you can stay healthy and if you eat In appropriate food combinations it can becomes the root cause of all physical and mental health issues.

She has covered basic fundamentals of Ayurveda with its unique relation with our food, it states, Food types everything with very easy to understand words. She has also included the herbs section of Ayurveda a perfect blending of Ayurveda in all aspects, and also covered Yoga, Meditation Mudra which are the sub branches of Ayurveda a complete blending of Holistic healing with body, Mind and Soul, I am very much sure that readers of this book will get everything what they want to know of perfect Holistic health system which born and brought up in India and now rapidly spreading across the globe. I congratulate Vaidya Aruna for such an informative book which is definitely going to be helpful to all health conscious people of the USA andwest. Again I appreciate her effort for spreading our science of life on a global platform and readers of this book will get a lots of information of this great science Ayurveda.

Lindy Sellers, Author, Artist, Teacher of Home Arts.

"In her book, Healing Mind, Body and Soul, Dr. Patki breaks down Ayurveda into bite-size pieces that anyone can understand. I have benefited greatly from her treatments and her cooking class at the Ayurveda Healing Spa; Having her book in hand helps to reinforce all of her teachings, and my health is so much better because of it. "

Anupama Kizhakkeveettil, Ph.D.

Vaidya Aruna Patki is an experienced US-based Ayurvedic Practitioner, who brings unique concepts into her teaching and clinical practice. In this book, she has captured modern contemplation of ancient concepts which will be useful for new aspirants of Ayurveda!

WHAT OUR CLIENTS SAY'S

I want to express my sincere appreciation to ArunaPatki and Ayurveda Healing Spa. I have been suffering with tinnitus for a few months following an ear infection...with very little relief in spite of trying many treatment modalities including acupuncture, chiropractic adjustments, craniosacral therapy, and conventional medicine. A forward thinking physician suggested I consult with Aruna, who made time for me in spite of her very busy schedule. We focused on each stage of Ayurveda's healing process beginning with Dinacharya, including asana, pranayama and meditation. The abhyanga and shirodhara were very beneficial - as was the steam detox following body work sessions. Aruna also taught me to eat and even cook aurvedically which I have been able to integrate into my daily routine. Aruna's skillful interventions have helped to lessen my symptoms, hopelessness and anxiety, for which I am forever grateful.

~ Cyntia, Psychologist , Tampa-Florida

Having exhausted western medicine with a chronic sinus issue, it was time to look for a more holistic avenue. In my search for a certified and licensed Ayurveda practitioner, I found Aruna Patki online. She was prompt in response to my email inquiry and very flexible with her schedule to accommodate my daily schedule. Based on the initial interview, she recommended the most suitable program for my body type and needs. During the weeklong detox program, I enjoyed a daily massage, targeted yoga and breathing instructions and a daily bag full of great tasting lunch and breakfast. The interaction with her quickly reveals that she knows what she is doing. I also had the pleasure of joining one of her cooking classes. She makes it look so easy with a contagious happy attitude resulting in great tasting food. The positive impact on my health and overall wellbeing was noticeable rather quickly. She can guide you through the program but you will have to take that first step.

~ Bernie

After visiting the Ayurveda Healing Spa, I realized I haven't experienced anything quite like it before. I have visited many different types of spas through my international travels but nothing like the experience at Ayurveda Healing Spa of Concord NC, Aruna Patki provided. Combining an evaluation, food choices and therapeutic massages, it really focuses on the entire person. I recognized traditional massage techniques, but also some very different ones as well. She has a very distinctive touch, light, yet deep so you can feel muscle movement. With a background in hospitality and teaching classes in spa management, it is always very interesting and exciting to learn about the different treatments and techniques so I can share them with my students. I was also amazed that even after several days, I feel a difference in my wellbeing, more clarity, focus, brightness. I am anxious to learn and experience more with ArunaPatki's help....Will recommend by heart.

~ Ann-Marie Weldon

" Being a doctor of homeopathy myself, it gave me a glimpse of how holistic your practice is.....'to offer and heal the individual and not the disease' resonates with homeopathic principle of healing as well. I've personally experienced great positive and spiritual growth through your sessions of 'Panchakarma' and am forever grateful for the friendly guidance that has aligned my life back to happy and healthy! Thanks ArunaPatki of Ayurveda Healing spa ,Concord NC for your guidance from the bottom of my heart!"

~ Anonymous. Charlotte Nc

How can I ever thank you? You have changed me and my life more than you could ever know. When I first came to you I had no idea that my healing would be so great or so swift, but such is the way of God, who definitely works through you. Thank you.

~ Maria

ArunaPatki an Ayurvedic Practitioner at "Ayurveda Healing Spa", is an amazingly intuitive Ayurvedic practitioner. After six years of chasing my

acid reflux symptoms, which culminated in bronchitis-like events where I unneedingly was prescribed anitbiotics, I feel like I've finally received

the help I needed. My symptoms have reduced by 90% in just five weeks. I felt relief of symptoms in two days. My digestive tract feels calmer, more peaceful, and like it is finally healing. I learned so much during the 10 day cleanse, and cooking class with Dr. Patki. I learned how to eat for my Pitta/Vata type, what kind of lifestyle changes I needed to make to support my ongoing health and healing, and the cleanse produced results that toxins were released. I can't say enough about Dr. Patki's abilities and warm bedside manner. She is a blessing in my life and I am so grateful to have been under her care! Thank you Dr. Patki for being you! Karen Pierce, Psychotherapist, Life and Leadership Coach, Charlotte, NC

~ Karen - Charlotte, NC

Having exhausted western medicine with a chronic sinus issue, it was time to look for a more holistic avenue. In my search for a certified and licensed Ayurveda practitioner, I found Aruna Patki online. She was prompt in response to my email inquiry and very flexible with her schedule to accommodate my daily schedule. Based on the initial interview, she recommended the most suitable program for my body type and needs. During the weeklong detox program, I enjoyed a daily massage, targeted yoga and breathing instructions and a daily bag full of great tasting lunch and breakfast. The interaction with her quickly reveals that she knows what she is doing. I also had the pleasure of joining one of her cooking classes. She makes it look so easy with a contagious happy attitude resulting in great tasting food. The positive impact on my health and overall wellbeing was noticeable rather quickly. She can guide you through the program but you will have to take that first step.

~ Bernie - NY,USA

I first learned about Ayurveda last summer and was very interested in the lifestyle. I read a few books on the subject and decided to dig deeper and look for an Ayurveda practitioner. I was so happy to find ArunaPatki (an Ayurveda physician from India) and her Ayurveda Healing Spa in the Charlotte area. I have been seeing ArunaPatki for about 2 ½ months now. I have (almost effortlessly) lost over 12 pounds. Even better than that, my blood pressure has gone from an average of 145/85 to an average of 105/60. I have also noticed that I feel much happier and I am more relaxed than I used to be. I believe this has everything to do with the panchakarma therapies, herbal supplements and teas, the diet that was given to me to balance my doshas and following a daily routine. I sincerely thank you ArunaPatki!

~ Mary - Dallas, NC

As a psychotherapist in private practice for over 15 years I understand the psychological impact stress creates on a person. After being diagnosed with breast cancer last June, I gained an even greater appreciation for the role physical illness plays in stress creation. I believe stress and illness can become vicious cycles and so I wanted a natural means to release stored stress. Even more importantly, I wanted a completely holistic way to detox my body from months of chemotherapy and radiation. I had a successful experience with Ayurvedic healing approximately 10 years ago, and so I immediately wanted to incorporate that into my healing journey. I went through a 6 day cleansing program with Dr. Patki and I saw results immediately; diminished pain, a significant increase in energy and clarity, and much sounder sleep. I whole-heartedly recommend Dr. Patki and the Ayurveda Healing Spa to anyone who wishes to heal from illness and/or create a solid foundation of health and well-being. I encourage you to follow her instructions faithfully and completely so you may fully embrace this gift of healing. I gained a lot of weight during chemotherapy due to steroids and appetite stimulants. I found the nutrition program to be very helpful and am losing weight and embracing a new lifestyle of eating which does NOT cause me to be hungry.

~ Suzanne Halstead Link, MA, LPC

About ten months ago, my daughter was diagnosed with a very serious condition known as ameloblastoma, a bone tumor that was precipitated by an impacted wisdom tooth. Though the tooth was extracted and the tumor enucleated, it eventually replicates and begins to feed on healthy tissue. We were told there is no recourse for this condition except for extremely invasive surgery. After trying innumerable naturopathic approaches, with no real results, we took her to the Ayurvedic Healing Spa, where she underwent the penetrating cleansing of the panchakarma treatment, and miraculously, the tumor began to recede. Since, she has had another panchakarma, and it is all but undetectable. We are beyond grateful for the results of the Ayurvedic approach to health and feel forever indebted to its wisdom. Dr. Patki's Ayurvedic Healing Spa was a blessing and we continually recommend it to everyone we know and meet.

~ Sankofa Charlotte, NC

I am a 68 year old man. I recently took part in the seven day cleansing program at doctor Patki's office - not knowing what to expect or if i should expect anything at all. Well, I am blown away with the results. My metabolism has gone from a 2 to a 8. That's just about perfect for me. This change took about three weeks. I highly recommend this program to everyone.

~ Roger

You may often encounter difficulties while juggling life's demands and taking care of your well-being. If you ask yourself the questions, "What does my body want?" and "What is good for me today?" you will know the answer almost immediately. The answers that come to mind when we ask these questions usually come in terms of things we should be omitting from our diet or lifestyle. However, despite our intuition, we often ignore the answers to these questions. Have you ever found yourself ignoring your own wisdom? Sometimes we even seek an external source when we are lost or confused — a magazine, a doctor, or a good friend who is following the current fad diet — thinking that everyone but us has answers! We still have this wisdom within ourselves, but we feel disconnected from it. Maybe we have forgotten that it is even there.

Ayurveda provides us with the tools needed to listen to our own wisdom again. It helps us to tap into the truth that is all around us and available through our body. The intention of this book is to help individuals attain knowledge for day-to-day ayurvedic health practices and build a healthier lifestyle and community. With consistent ayurvedic practices and knowledge, one may teach one's children to listen to their bodies, right from an early age and through their lives. Ayurveda can help you, your family, and your community to live in balance and to achieve harmony in body, mind, and spirit (the inner you).

Ayurveda uses habits to create the health and vitality that we want and need throughout our lives. Our habits can bring us balance on a consistent basis, which will work like medicine if we allow this process to take action in our lives.

DISCLAIMER

This book is intended for educational purposes only. It is not intended as a substitute for the diagnosis or treatment provided by a licensed health practitioner or a physician's medical recommendation. Statements and information in this book about health conditions or guidelines regarding ayurvedic therapies have not been recommended by the U.S. food and drug administration. This book is not intended to identify, treat, or diagnose any health conditions and is provided as an example of authentic traditional ayurvedic practice guideline for health and well-being.

Published By,
Vaidya Aruna Patki (Doctor of Ayurvedic Medicine)
Copyright 2019 Ayurveda Healing Spa LLC
No production allowed in whole or in part or any other forms by any electronic or mechanical
means without the written permission by the Ayurveda Healing Spa.
Cover Design Lay-out-By Aruna Patki (On Elemental Theory Concepts).
For more information on Ayurveda contact,
Ayurveda Healing Spa,
Ayurvedic Panchkarma (Detox), Mind-Body-soul Health Center
Internal & External Beauty & Healing Center,
754 Barossa Valley Drive,
Concord , NC 28027
001-704 808 0708

Table of Contents

Let Ayurveda help you improve your quality of life and restore the balance and harmony of your mind, body, and soul.

PART 1
AYURVEDIC THEORY

Habits and Their Role in Creating You

It takes at least 30 days to create a new habit. Creating a new habit means we are creating a new groove in our consciousness. Do we want to create a line in the sand or a deep groove into clay? The difference has to do with the intention, attention, and commitment we put into the habits we create. Unhealthy habits are always the easiest to set in because they often take less effort. We get used to thinking a certain way, or engaging in a certain routine in our life because that's just the way it always has been and we don't question it. At times our habits can become degenerative to the body. Humans are designed to refine our habits as we get older- to get more intelligent and in tune with our consciousness. However, we often find ourselves taking the opposite route in today's world. We have lost touch with our innate wisdom.

We often seek answers outside of ourselves. What should I have for lunch? What foods should I incorporate or omit from my diet? How large should my meals be... how many meals should I have today? What does the latest science tell me about how my diet and lifestyle should look? These are all important questions that we seem to ask everyone else but ourselves! The answer to what you should omit from your diet is in the feeling you have after you eat certain foods. If foods with certain qualities make you feel vibrant, and tap into something you love about life, that is something you need to have more in your diet. Eat more foods with those qualities. If a food gives you congestion and allergy symptoms, or a feeling of sluggishness and heaviness after you eat, maybe you find yourself thinking 'I don't want to do that anymore'. The answer is within you! If we get into the habit of continuing to consume meals without mindfulness or connection to our food, we will find our physiology getting dense, less toned, and weak. If we begin to pause before we eat and after we eat to notice how we feel and notice what comes up to our consciousness regarding our food, we begin to take the direction of becoming more in tune and intelligent with consciousness and the world around us.

Learning to create habits that will up level our digestion, spiritual practice, emotional health, and physical health, is a journey we usually have to make a little at a time. Have you ever tried to make large, sweeping changes to your lifestyle with the aim of bettering yourself and, three days in, wonder how it all collapsed so quickly? Our previous habits have rooted us into a particular place in our lives. This place is not one we can be uprooted from immediately. In fact, we don't have to be uprooted at all. A little at a time we can soften the ground around us, redirect our roots and settle into a place that is nourishing for what we need.

Through small changes to your diet and lifestyle at a time, you can obtain optimal health and teach yourself how to achieve balance in your life. The lovely thing about Ayurveda is that the more you study and practice it the easier it becomes. In this book we will teach you how to shift your habits a little at a time, how to improve your diet for your body type, how to use breath and yoga asanas (postures) to influence your consciousness and physiology, and how to know which of these things YOU need and when.

"Self-victory guideline through Ayurveda."

Chapter 1: Healthy Eating - The Ayurvedic Perspective

How to Eat Is More Important than What You Eat

What is health?

Health has been defined as *"the absence of illness or injury."* While this has come to be the consensus in the allopathic medical community, the Ayurvedic tradition defines health as *"one whose soul, mind, and sense organs are all in a state of equilibrium."* It is the Ayurvedic definition of health that we shall cover in this work.

How to Eat > What You Eat

How to eat is more important than what we eat. Food consumed with awareness and respect contribute to bodily wellness. On the other end of the spectrum, food consumed without awareness and respect lead to digestive disturbances. Awareness simply means the utilization of the senses while eating.

Ex: Do you ever find yourself looking at your phone while consuming a meal? Or gazing at the television at a restaurant while eating? The next time you catch yourself doing this, take a break from the screen and truly immerse yourself in your eating experience. Next time you sit down to eat, see if you can notice the smell of the food, the colors in the food, or the texture of food. Then see what flavors and tastes you can pick out with each bite. Observe your chewing. Are you chewing enough? Notice if you can eat your food with love, rather than disgust. Or, practice eating sitting down at the table, rather than running out the door.

The senses and their role in food consumption are as follows:

- **Smell:** Just as essential oils can have an aromatic therapeutic effect on the individual, so can the food that we consume. For example, the aroma of certain foods may trigger memories of a loved one or a memorable family function may come to mind as well as the loving energy and environment associated with it. This can bring one to a higher frequency that may facilitate the proper assimilation and digestion of food. Also, the smell of the food will determine its freshness.

- **Taste:** The way food tastes is usually a good indicator of whether or not it is edible. However, just because a particular food tastes good doesn't necessarily mean that it is good for you. Most important to consider is this… is it sweet to the taste, yet bitter to the body?

- **Touch:** Healing touch everyday with the Ayurvedic self-massage will bring the health and wellbeing sense to the body. It helps to release toxins and enhance the immune function, improve circulation and induce sleep. So love yourself. Am I doing my massage on regular basis?
- **Sight:** This includes its visual presentation, as well as visualizing the benefit(s) the body receives through ingestion.

- **Hearing:** Listening to what the body is communicating to you through the process; i.e., How is this food contributing to my wellness? Do I really require this nourishment at this time? Am I eating based on habit or needs?

"Asatomaasadgamaya
Tamasomaajyotirgamaya
Mṛityormaaamṛitamgamaya
Om shaantiḥshaantiḥshaantiḥ"

"From the unreal, lead us to the Real; from darkness, lead us unto Light; from death, lead us to Immortality. Om peace, peace, peace."

Next, I would like to start with the first concept which is extremely important in our day to day life is

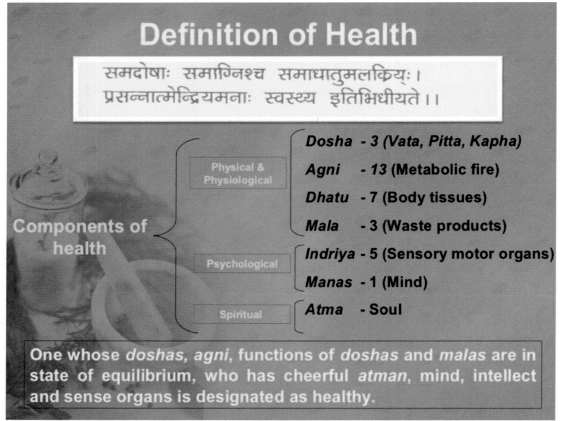

achieving Health. We will focus on the definition of optimal health from an Ayurvedic perspective

Bhagavad Gita 6:16-17

"O Arjuna! The gourmand, the scanty eater, the person who habitually oversleeps, the one who sleeps too little --- none of these finds success in yoga. (16) He who with [proper] regularity eats, relaxes, works, sleeps, and remains awake will find yoga the destroyer of suffering. (17)"

Food + (awareness/respect) = well bodies

Food − (awareness/respect) = digestive disturbances
Awareness = utilization of the senses while eating

Qualities/Gunas

For any and everything we experience in our lives, whether it be food, locations, beliefs, or physical items, there are qualities that help define them. Think of the foods you eat on a daily basis… how would you describe them? Some adjectives may come to mind such as- hot, gooey, crisp, spicy, heavy, comforting, etc. depending on the food that you eat. Ayurveda uses these qualities as measuring tools to figure out where to find balance in our lives. This is very simple. An example would be- if you feel heavy and sluggish, you need more things in your life that will increase light quality. On the other hand, if you feel like you have excess light quality (maybe very light foods, not enough structure and stability in your life) then you may need to add more into your life that has heavy quality. Shita (cold) vs Ushna (hot) measures temperature. Snigdha (oily) vs Ruksha (dry) measure moisture. Guru (heavy) vs Laghu (light) measures weight of something. Sthula (gross) vs Sukshma (subtle) measures materialization of something. Sandra (dense) vs Drava (liquid) measures viscosity of something.

Below I list several qualities, which will help you understand Ayurvedic principles throughout this book.

- <u>Shita</u>- cold, winter, ice water. What does cold do? It solidifies and hardens things.
- <u>Ushna</u>- hot, summer, boiling water. What does hot do? It liquifies, melts, and softens things. It helps digest things.
- <u>Snigdha</u>- oily. In Sanskrit, the word 'Sneha' means both oil and love. What a powerful word! The bon
- Ruksha- dry
- Guru- heavy
- Laghu- light
- Sthula- gross
- Sukshma- subtle
- Sandra - dense
- Drava- liquid

- Mrudu- soft
- Kathina- hard
- Sthira- static
- Chala- mobile
- Picchila- sticky (dense)
- Vishada- clear
- Slackshna- slimy
- Khara- rough
- Manda- slow
- Tikshna- sharp

Rules

- **Meal blessing/offering:** Blessing a meal before consumption raises its vibrational frequency. This is to be done prior to providing it as an offering to the Divine within. After all, when dedicating something to the Divine, you always want to ensure that it's the best that you have to offer.

    "The items we use to feed ourselves are Brahma. The food itself is Brahma. The fire of hunger we feel is Brahma. We are Brahma and the process of eating and digesting the food is the action of Brahma. Finally, the result we obtain is Brahma."

- **Peaceful environment (outer and inner):**
- **Adequate chewing:** While there are different sources indicating specific, and often, conflicting number of times to properly chew food, the overall rule of thumb is to chew until the food becomes liquefied.
- **Never eat until full:** Eat until 75% full, make sure you have 25% of your stomach empty at the end of the meal. Do not eat until you are completely full!
- **Allow time for digestion:** It takes approximately six to eight hours for food to pass through the stomach and small intestine. This times varies between individuals and between men and women.

Below is an example blessing over the meal. You could incorporate a blessing from your own culture or belief system that resonates with you.

Meal Blessing
AumSahaNaavavatu
Saha Nau Bhunaktu
SahaVeeryamKaravaavahai
TejasvinaaVadheetamastu
MaaVidvishaaVahai ||
ShantihShantihShantih ||

"Let us protect each other. Let us eat together. Let us work together. Let us study together to be bright and successful. Let us not hate each other. Aum Peace, Peace, Peace."

NOTABLE QUOTE

"There is no official coronation ceremony held to declare the lion king of the jungle. He becomes king by his own attributes and heroic actions."

"The sun looks alike while rising and setting. Great men too remain alike in both good and bad times."

Tips

- **Drink moderately**
- **Room temperature liquids are best:** Cold fluids can shock the system.
- **Digestion peaks around noon:** The digestive fire (agni- lesser light) is in sync with the planetary fire (sun- greater light).
- Allow <u>at least three hours</u> between meals

The mind of the cook is commensurate with the energy and quality of the food. Consider this when eating a meal not prepared by yourself; i.e. "eating out".

Mind of the cook = energy in the food

Foods and Habits That Increase Vibration

Organically grown whole foods, local, seasonal fruits, vegetables, nuts, and seeds

Foods and Habits That Decrease Vibration

Genetically modified, processed, junk or fast foods: anything containing hydrogenated oils (including palm, canola, or vegetable oil

Preparing meals with love and intention	Refined carbohydrates, sugar, fried foods, non-organic dairy and meat
Blessing the food and all who made it possible for your nourishment and pleasure	Using a microwave, which kills the living enzymes in the food
Consuming your meal while seated, mindfully Chewing each mouthful	Eating until full eating when distracted, angry, tense, or upset

Bhagavad Gita 14:9-13

"Sattva attaches one to happiness; rajas to activity; and tamas, by eclipsing the power of discrimination, to miscomprehension. (9) Sometimes sattva is predominant, overpowering rajs and tamas; sometimes rajas prevails, not sattva or tamas; and sometimes tamas obscures sattva and rajas. (10) One may know that sattva is prevalent when the light of wisdom shines through all the sense gates of the body. (11) Preponderance of rajas causes greed, activity, undertaking of works, restlessness, and desire. (12) Tamas as the ruling guna produces darkness, sloth, neglect of duties, and delusion. (13)"

How do I determine my dosha type/prakruti?

VATTA

Element: Air& Space

Qualities:

(+) active, rough, creative, light, cold, subtle, mobile, communication

(-) anxiety, dryness, constipation

Locations: colon, thighs, bones, joints, ears, skin, brain, nerve tissues

Physiology: related to movement

- Breathing
- Talking
- Nerve impulses
- Muscle/tissue movements
- Circulation
- Assimilation of food
- Elimination
- Urination

- Menstruation

Psychology:

- communication
- creativity
- flexibility
- quickness of thought

Keywords: grounding, warming, routine

> (+) warm foods and spices

> (-) raw and cold foods; extreme cold and wind

Routine:

(+)

- engage in wholesome and contemplative activities (spending time in nature)
- go to bed early
- meditate daily
- yoga, tai chi, swimming, walking

(-)

- eating while nervous/ anxious or depressed
- eating on the run
- alcohol, coffee or black tea
- cigarette smoking
- irregular routine
- going to bed late at night

PITTA

Element: fire and water

Qualities: digestion and metabolism; oily, sharp, hot, light, moving, liquid and acidic

Locations: small intestines, stomach, liver, spleen, pancreas, blood, eyes, sweat

Physiology: provides body with heat and energy

- governs processes related to conversion and transformation throughout mind and body
- infection, inflammation, rashes, ulcer, fever, heartburn

Psychology:

(+) governs joy, courage, willpower, anger, jealousy, mental perception intellect

(-) overheat

Keywords: cooling, calming, moderation

  (-) hot spices, salt, excessive oil, excessive steam, artificial stimulants

Routine:

(+)

- meditate daily
- yoga, tai chi, swimming, walking

(-)

- eating while angry
- black tea, coffee, alcohol
- cigarettes
- over working
- overly compulsive

KAPHA

Element: Earth &Water

Qualities:

Keywords: drying, stimulating expression

(+)

- focus on non-attachment in daily life
- regular emotional housekeeping
- make time for introspective activities (writing, meditation)
- distinguish between being nice and being taken advantage of
- go to bed early

(-)

- luxurious, leisurely lifestyle
- heavy foods/drinks
- fat/ oily foods

- overeating
- eating when depressed
- too much time in cool damp climates
- not engaging in physical activity
- spending most of the time indoors
- avoiding intellectual challenges

Doshas and the seasons

In Ayurveda changes of season are termed as Ritucharya. While changing seasons of nature, there will be corresponding effects on the panchmahabhutas/five elements and thereby the doshas of body [Vata, Pitta, Kapha].

SEASON	SUMMER	FALL	LATE SPRING/ EARLYWINTER
Dosha	Pitta	Vata	Kapha
Seasonal	Perspiration,	Dry skin,	Lethargy, weight gain
Imbalance Water	Rashes, inflammation, irritability, excess oil	Constipation, insomnia, anxiety retention	Oversleeping, congestion, bloating
Eat More	Cool, refreshing foods (watermelon and cucumber	Warming, moist food (soups and grains)	Warming foods (cooked greens, berries, and spices)
Eat Less	Spicy food, coffee, sugar, chocolate, alcohol	Dry crisp foods (crackers, salads); cold drinks; smoothies	Excess carbs, dairy, wheat

We can bring the transformations and changes in us by simply following the **"HAPPY"** protocol.

H = Heat. Natural sun, steams, candles, fireplaces steams, saunas can all be helpful to the sense of touch and balances out the darkness by providing the light. Taking a walk, or run in nature, depending upon weather and timings, can all be helpful as per your intentions and body type.

A = Aromatic oil. The sense of smell pleases the mind and balances the energy of the Kaphadosha. Aromatic oil diffusers, or steams with aromatic oils create the atmosphere which will be very relaxing and calming. Sandalwood, citrus, gardenia, jasmine are good to enhance and uplift moods.

P = Play. Every day you have to move, walk or play enough to produce a sweat and create a heat, and warmth in you .Music, dance, yoga, and walking are few to do on regular basis where you connect your mind and body.

P = Pretty. Always look at the beautiful, natural things around you as like the same way you see the pretty things within you. Flowers, fruits, and nature are examples. It is also helpful to take care of indoor or outdoor plants, and flowers. The colors all add up and enhance the vibrations and our eyes feels happy when we look at these things. When our eyes see beauty our minds feel happy, too. And our eyes are location of Pittadosha or energy so it balances the Pitta.

Y = Yummy/means enhancing mood food which is sattvic. This type of food brings joyfullness, calmness, and patience, which will help to promote the calmness and harmony within us. Ayurveda teaches, there is a mind -body-soul connection.

UpakarahparodharmahpraytnodaiVatam param.
Sushilata para nitihkaryamsamghatmakam param.

"Service is the greatest virtue. Effort is the highest fortune. Noble character is the ultimate wisdom and the greatest work is of organization of the society."

Oh, God give us food which does not cause any disease and also gives us strength. Atharved

He, who takes food in proper measure lives a long life and lives without disease, gets strength and alertness of mind. However, his children are born healthy and without any deformity or disease. Mahabharat

Food types

Bhagavad Gita 17:7-10

> *"Each of the three classes of men even likes one of the three kinds of foods; so also their yajnas, penances, and almsgivings. Hear thou about these distinctions. (7) Foods that promote longevity, vitality, endurance, health, cheerfulness, and good appetite; and that are savory, mild, substantial, and agreeable to the body, are liked by pure-minded (sattvic) persons. (8) Foods that are bitter, sour, salty, excessively hot, pungent, harsh, and burning are preferred by rajasic men; and produce pain, sorrow, and disease. (9) Foods that are nutritionally worthless, insipid, putrid, stale, refuse, and impure are enjoyed by tamasic persons. (10)"*

Food type is based on the three gunas or qualities. They are sattvic, rajasic, and tamasic. Following is a brief description of each.

Sattvic- "pure essence"; mind calming

Bhagavad Ghita 14:6

"O Sinless One (Arjuna)! Of these three gunas, the stainless sattva gives enlightenment and health. Nevertheless, it binds man through attachment to happiness and attachment to knowledge."

Al Qur'an 2:168, 172

"O men! Eat the lawful and good things out of what is in the earth, and do not follow the footsteps of the Shaytan; surely he is your open enemy. (168)O you who believe! Eat of the good things that We have provided you with, and give thanks to Allah if Him it is that you serve. (172)"

- whole grains such as brown rice, whole wheat, millet, corn, soybeans, lentils, oats and beans
- fresh fruits and vegetables

Rajasic- "can-do energy"; mind agitating

Bhagavad Gita 14:7

"O Son of Kunti (Arjuna), understand that the activating rajas is imbued with passion, giving birth to desire and attachment; it strongly binds the embodied soul by a clinging to works."

- fish and meat (salmon, sole, trout, lamb, chicken, turkey, tuna, venison, eggs)

Leviticus 11:10-12

"And all that have not fins and scales in the seas, and in the rivers, of all that move in the

waters, and of any living thing which is in the waters, they shall be an abomination unto you: (10) They shall be even an abomination unto you; ye shall not eat of their flesh, but ye shall have their carcases in abomination. (11) Whatsoever hath no fins nor scales in the waters, that shall be an abomination unto you. (12)"

- spices (salt, black pepper, cayenne, and ginger); onions radishes, garlic

- stimulants (coffee, tea, sugar, cola drinks and chocolate in moderation, beer and wine)

Tamasic- "dark and dull"; mind dulling

Bhagavad Gita 14:8

"O Bharata (Arjuna)! Know that tamas arises from ignorance, deluding all embodied beings. It binds them by misconception, idleness, and slumber."

- beef and veal, hotdogs, sausages, sardines, bologna, bacon, ham
- deep fried foods such as french fries
- foods preserved with salt or pickled vinegar
- hard liquor and other mixed drinks
- mind filled with dark emotions (anger, jealousy, greed)
- overeating

These foods and behaviors do not benefit mind or body, and destroy the body's immunity.

Now can we practice how we can overcome the food cravings or addictions? Your own practice and practice for few weeks or months will likely bring a change in you. Have patience and observe the changes and listen to your voice or inner call of the body.

This is a picture of an Ayurvedic meal. This demonstrates the importance of colors in the food. For example, different colors can nourish the body in different ways. It is also importance to eat carbohydrates with proteins, vegetables, and dairy (e.g., freshly made yogurt or buttermilk).

Our plate at least should look like this. A small portion of meat and dairy with large portion of fruits and vegetables and grains and lentils. The meat percentage should be like a small, side dish.

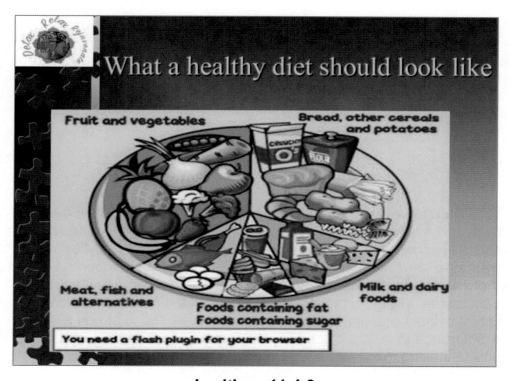

Leviticus 11:4-8

"Nevertheless these shall ye not eat of them that chew the cud, or of them that divide the hoof: as <u>the camel</u>, because he cheweth the cud, but divideth not the hoof; <u>he is unclean unto you.</u> (4) And <u>the coney,</u> because he cheweth the cud, but divideth not the hoof; <u>he is unclean unto you.</u> (5) And <u>the hare,</u> because he cheweth the cud, but divideth not the hoof; <u>he is unclean unto you.</u> (6) And <u>the swine,</u> though he divide the hoof, and be cloven footed, yet he cheweth not the cud; <u>he is unclean to you.</u> (7) <u>Of their flesh shall ye not eat, and their carcase shall ye not touch; they are unclean to you.</u> (8)"

The Six Tastes

Have you ever watched a baby bite into a wedge of lemon? The baby usually puckers up and is so surprised by the sour taste that their body has an immediate reaction to it! The baby will push the lemon away; however, after they notice the sweet aftertaste of the lemon, they may grab towards it and want to take another bite. This is a perfect example of how the taste of our food affects us. Western culture has done an excellent job of mastering three of the six tastes- sweet, sour, and salty. Think of the food you eat on a regular basis- can you pinpoint at least one or more of these tastes in what you eat on a daily basis? Now, think of the bitterness in a cup of coffee, or even in a leaf of spinach. Now think of the pungency you feel biting into a hot pepper, feeling your head and face get hot and maybe starting to sweat a little. Now, think of the rough feeling in your mouth after having a tart drink of cranberry juice- that is astringency. Each of the six tastes have qualities and unique physiological responses that come with them.

Ayurveda believes that, to have a balanced life, we must have each of the tastes. Each meal should include all six of the tastes in appropriate amounts. Tastes are the emotions of the body. Have you ever noticed that you crave different foods depending on your mood? Or, on the other hand, maybe you notice that the foods you eat cause an emotional response in you. Each taste causes a specific reaction in the body. Too much of one taste may throw your body and emotions out of balance.

For each taste we will have:

Where the taste buds for this taste are, the emotions associated with it, the qualities (gunas) associated with it, what a deficiency of this taste looks like, what excess of this taste looks like

The next section focuses on how to create meals including all six tastes and indicates proper amounts of each taste in a meal.

According to Ayurvedic medicine, there are six tastes associated with the different types of food.
They are:

- **Sweet**- This taste promotes nourishment and strength to all tissues. Ex. Fruits, Beet, Carbs, potatoes, nuts, rice, bread, grains, oils, meat, etc.

- **Salty**- This taste maintains or brings balances (such as electrolytes).Ex. Rock, regular, Sea, black etc.

- **Sour**- This taste stimulates to ignites the digestive power. Ex. Orange, lemon, tomato, berries, vinegar, alcohol, etc.

- **Pungent**- This taste improves the digestive activity and absorption activity. Ex. Onion, Garlic, cayenne, pepper, black pepper, jalepenos, radish, etc.

- **Bitter**- This taste stimulates all the tastes. Ex. Broccoli, cauliflower, asparagus, leafy greens, cabbage, turmeric, coffee, rhubarb, etc.

- **Astringent**- This taste stimulates all the tastes. Ex. Broccoli, cauliflower, asparagus, leafy greens, cabbage, turmeric, coffee, rhubarb, etc.

The 6 Tastes

Sweet

Sour

Salty

Pungent

Bitter

Astringent

Dosha-Balancing Tastes

- Vata - sweet, sour, salty
- Pitta-sweet, bitter, astringent
- Kapha-pungent, bitter, astringent

Sweet increases Kapha and decreases Vata/Pitta
Sour increases Pitta/Kapha and decreases Vata
Salty increases Pitta/Kapha and decreases Vata
Pungent increases Vata/Pitta and decreases Kapha
Bitter increases Vata and decreases Pitta/Kapha
Astringent increases Vata and decreases Pitta/Kapha.

Below is a demonstration of this concept.

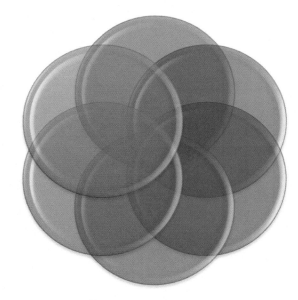

Sweet
- Cold, Wet & Heavy
- P/V decreased
- K increased

Astringent
- Cold, Dry & Heavy
- P/K decreased
- V increased

Sour
- Hot, Wet & Light
- V decreased
- P/K increased

Bitter
- Cold, Dry & Light
- P/K decreased
- V increased

Salty
- Hot, Wet & Heavy
- V decreased
- P/K increased

Pungent
- Hot, Dry & Light
- K decreased
- V/P increased

Energies and the elemental combinations.

Sweet -Earth, Water

Sour -Earth, Fire

Salty -Fire, Water

Pungent –Fire, Air

Bitter -Air, Ether

Astringent-Air, Earth

Food Cravings And Rajas, Tamas, Sattva

Do you remember being curious about the cup of coffee in your parent's hand as a child? Perhaps you remember taking your first drink of coffee ever and immediately making a face, deciding to not have any more of that bitter stuff!! Has your taste for coffee changed as you have gotten older? Take a moment and notice how your tastes may have changed since you were a child. Are there any changes you have noticed? Usually, cravings are healthy. They are your body trying to get back into balance! Have you ever noticed yourself craving a light, crisp salad after a few days of eating heavier foods? Craving a hot, hearty soup when the weather gets cold and dry? You probably aren't craving that same hot soup when the weather is hot and humid.

UpakarahparodharmahpraytnodaiVatam param.
Sushilata para nitihkaryamsamghatmakam param.

"Service is the greatest virtue. Effort is the highest fortune. Noble character is the ultimate wisdom and the greatest work is of organization of the society."

PANCHA MAHABHOOTAS
Five elements = five primordial

AYURVEDA DOSHA OVERVIEW	Vata	Pita	KapHa
Energy of -	Movement kinetic energy	Transformation thermal energy	Stability potential energy
Elements -	Air+ Ether	Fire + Water	Earth + Water
Means -	'to move'	'to burn'	'to stick'
In the body responsible for -	All movements of the body, mind & senses and the process of elimination.	Heat, energy production, metabolism & digestive functions.	Physical stability, proper body structure, resistance and fluid balance.
Particular Qualities -	Dry, Cold, Light, Irregular, Quick, Mobile, Rough, Rarefield	Oily, Hot, light, intense, sharp, fluid, liquid, acidic	Oily, cold, heavy, stable, dull, viscous, smooth, dense.
Seasons -	Late autumn early winter	Late spring summer	Late winter early spring
Time of day -	2-6am & 2-6pm	10-2am & 10-2pm	6-10am to 6-10pm
Life phase -	Old age catabolism	Adulthood metabolism	Childhood anabolism
Seats of the dosha in the body -	Large intestine, pelvic cavity, bones, skin, ears and thighs	Small intestine, stomach, sweat glandss, blood, fat, eys & skin	Chest,throat, head sinuses, nose, mouth, stomach, joints, plasma, mucus

Living things have jivatma
- Jivatma (individual soul) ------- Paratma (cosmic soul)

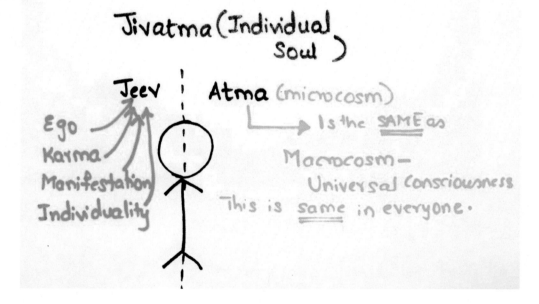

PARAMTMA (COSMIC SOUL)

Ayurvedic Trinity = trigunas/ tridoshas

ORIGIN OF AYURVEDA

The true history of Ayurveda starts from the time of the Holy books, the Vedas. Ancient mythology contends that the concept and essence of Ayurveda was revealed by the creator of the world himself – Lord Brahma.

INTRODUCTION OF AYURVEDA

It is said that they received their training of Ayurveda through direct cognition during meditation. In other words, the knowledge of the use of various methods of healing, prevention, longevity and surgery came through Divine revelation (Cosmic Intelligence); there was no guessing or testing and harming animals. These revelations were transcribed from the oral tradition into book form, interspersed with the other aspects of life and spirituality.

BHAGAVAD GITA 14:5

"O Mighty-armed (Arjuna)! The gunas inherent in Prakriti --- sattva, rajas, and tamas --- imprison in the body the Imperishable Dweller."

- Basic principles of Ayurveda apply to ALL humans

The Study Of One Science Cannot Give Definite And Perfect Knowledge Of The Related Subject!

ATTRIBUTES OF AYURVEDA

1) Well-balanced

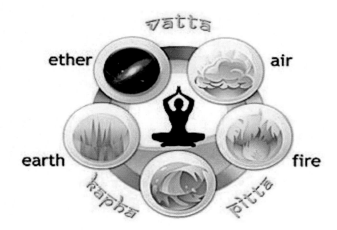

2) Holistic approach: The constitution and mental make-up of the INDIVIDUAL are taken into account when performing a diagnosis. This is done because Ayurveda recognizes that what may have caused a disease in one individual may be the result of a different root in another. Take for example, two individuals suffering from kidney disease. One individual may have the disease as a result of uncontrolled diabetes, while another may have it as a result of excessive sexual activity. Though the

imbalance manifests in the same organ, the initial cause or source of the problem is different. It is the cause that Ayurvedic medicine concerns itself with rather than merely addressing the symptoms.

3) Ayurveda is the first medical science in the world that knows the importance of the mind in maintaining perfect health. Ayurveda understands the vital role of the mind as anetiological factor in the creation and curing of disease, and recognizes that mind and body are one. For example, in some cases, cancer can be the result of stagnant physical or emotional trauma. Diabetes, can be the result of a conflict or feeling under attack by circumstances in the home or abroad, and the individual may be unable to cope or communicate their feelings at the time and/or process this in a healthy way. Kidney disease may be the result of a person overlooking and ignoring resentment. The more sluggish a person, the more toxic the kidneys become.

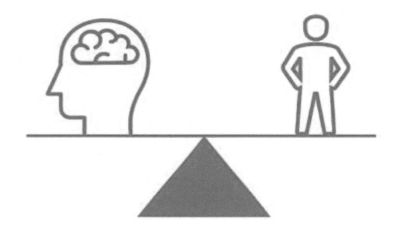

***If you want to see what your thoughts were like yesterday look at your body today. If you want to see what your body will be like tomorrow look at your thoughts today.* Indian Proverb**

4) Recognizes mind as the bridge between soul and the physical body

5) Finds that the quality of mind is greatly affected by the type of food you eat

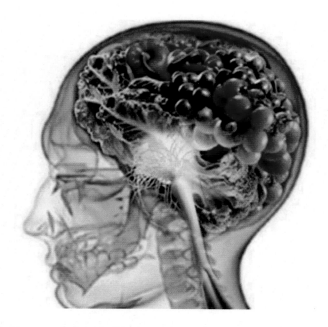

6) Believes in the existence of the spiritual dimension of humans; i.e., the soul can be instrumental in prevention and curing imbalances and disturbances in the body. Thus, the benefits of such practices such as yoga meditation, tai chi, reiki, etc.

7) Ayurvedic philosophy includes:
   a) Concept of trigunas

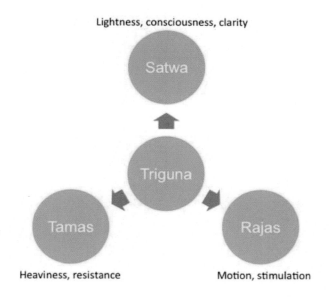

b) Five pentads/ The five elements of the body.

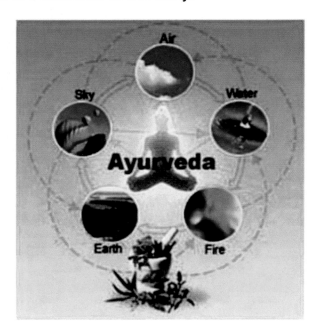

c) Tridoshas

Samadoshasamagnischasamadhatumalakriya.
Prasannatmendriyamanaswasthyaitiabhidiyate.

"The harmony of dosha (bio-energy), dhatu (fundamental/support of body structure), mala (bodily waste) and agni (metabolic fire), Happiness and Harmony in Soul, Sensory Organs, Mind is termed to be Healthy (mental and physical)."

Dosha	Nature Relationship	When Balanced	Imbalances
Kapha Larger build, strong, oily pale skin, thick hair, dislikes damp cold weather.	*Elements:* Water and earth	*Mind:* calm, reflection, love, nurturing, compassion, patience.	*Mind:* greed, envy, holds grudges, attachment.
Feed your dosha: Meals at 8a, 1p, 4p, and 6p. Early sleep, early rising. Exercise. Avoid heavy oily foods, dairy, and iced drinks.	*As in Nature:* Moon/Rain Late Winter Early Spring	*Body:* builds, strengthens, nourishes, protects, fat, fluids, reproduction.	*Body (problems of water):* congestion, obesity, allergies, lethargy, sinus problems.
Pitta Medium build, fair/reddish skin, fine straight hair, dislikes hot weather.	*Elements:* Fire and water	*Mind:* intelligence, concentration, memory, discrimination.	*Mind:* anger, hate, jealousy, controlling, hot temper.
Feed your dosha: Meals at 7a, noon, 3p and 6p. Daily meditation after 6 p.m. Avoiding heat, oil, salt, and exercise during cool part of day.	*As in Nature:* Sun/Heat Late Spring Summer	*Body:* metabolism, digestion, eyes, blood, skin, brain, heart.	*Body (problems of fire):* fevers, acid reflux, heartburn, acne, hypertension, nausea, migraines, endometriosis.
Vata Small, thin, lightest build, dry hair, crooked or protruding teeth, dislikes cold weather.	*Elements:* Air and space	Mind: imagination, restless, creative, spiritual, tranquility.	*Mind:* fear, anxiety, stress, worry, poor memory.
Feed your dosha: Meals at 7a, noon, 4p, and 6p. Naps 2-4p. Keeping warm. Maintaining calm. Avoid raw, cold foods. Regular routine.	*As in Nature:* Wind Fall Early Winter	*Body:* flexibility, blood flow, nerve impulses, fast in actions, emotions	*Body (problems of air):* pneumonia, hyperactivity, dry skin, constipation, gas, arthritis.

8) Local abnormality
   a) May be structural and/or functional

Increased/spoiled tridosha occupying weak/debilitated organ/tissue = disease of that tissue

Normal organ/tissue = disease-free

- Prakriti- nature of food articles
- Karana- method of processing

- Samyoga- combination

- Rashi- quantity
- Desha- habitat
- Kala- time
- Upayogasamstha- rules governing food intake
- Upayoktru- wholesomeness to individual who takes it

9) Agni concept: Agni is the digestive fire that facilitates digestion.

Weaker agni = weaker digestion/metabolic processes
Incomplete/abnormal digestion = formation of ama

Increased ama infects doshas = spoils them = toxicity = increased severity of disease(s)

Treatment = accumulated element of causative dosha
eliminated by first increasing power of
agni to normal function;
then treatment is directed to reduce the increased
quantity of the related dosha

10) Panchakarma:
- Vaman (vomiting)
- Virechana (purging)
- Basti (enema)
- Raktamoshana (blood letting)

- Nasya (medicated drug in nostrils)

EVOLVMENT OF LIFE

A) Swabhav- natural property of a substance
B) Eeshwan- almighty (God)
C) Yadruchcha- unknown cause
D) Niyati- fate
E) Parinaama- result, outcome, consequence

INDIAN PHILOSOPHY AND AYURVEDA

A) Theory of rebirth
B) Respects theories of creation of the universe
C) Charaka mentions

- Individual is represented by soul principle as in Advait philosophy
- Individual is composed of five elements as proposed in Vaisheshik philosophy
- Man is composed of 24 elements of Prakuti and Purush as proposed by Sankhya school

D) Inanimate and animate objects are created by combination of various ways minute indivisible particles of the five elements
E) This process = karmaphalas
F) When these fruits of action are immature and are abeyance, these particles start separating from each other until complete dissolution results; pralaya
G) Acknowledges God
H) Synthesis of Charaka, Sushruti, Vagbhata, etc

THEORY OF CREATION

*SAMKHYA = sam "thoroughly" + khya "to know"

1) Purusha- origin of all vitality; All-Knowing principle
2) Prakruti- omnipresent; without beginning or end
3) Mahat- universal form of knowledge; universal intelligence
   - sattvic
   - rajasic
   - tamasic
4) Ahankara- self-awareness

STAGES IN CREATION

Five pentads
- Akash (space) – ear; no movement or taste; intestinal tract, blood vessels, lymphatics, intercellular spaces, vacuum anywhere in the body

- Vayu (air) – contains oxygen, movement; touch, skin; gaseous components, pulsations
- Agni teja (energy)- lightness, roughness, hotness, dryness, luminosity; vision; eyes
- Ap (water)- tongue; taste, blood, urine, sweat, semen, stool
- pruthvi (earth)

1) Prakruti + purush = disturbed trigunas (active raja)
    rajoguna + satvaguna = mahat principles of sattva guna (intelligence)

2) First sattva guna dominated, then rajoguna, finally tamaguna. Then self-awareness (ahankar) arose.

3) Ahankara is of three types: satvic, rajasic, tamasic
   a) Satvicahankara corresponds to the five senses
   b) Rajasic corresponds to the five organs of action: speech, hands, feet, anus, and sex organs. These in turn are controlled by five vatdoshas (prana, udana, vyaana, samana and apana components of the nervous system)
   c) Satvic + rajasic correspond to states of mind
   d) Rajasic ahankara is incited by five basic elements (senses)
   e) Subtle body is born; mahat is born
      - Consists of five senses, five motor centers, five pranas, mind, ahankara, and intellect

Samkhya Philosophy of Creation

Purusha is unmanifested, formless, passive, beyond attributes, beyond cause and effect, space and time. Purusha is Pure Existence. *Prakruti* is the creative force of action, the source of form, manifestation, attributes and nature. *Mahad* is the cosmic Intelligence or Buddhi. *Ahamkar* is ego, the sense of "I am.". *Satva* is stability, pure aspect, awakening, essence and light. Rajas is dynamic movement. *Tamas* is static. It is potential energy, inertia, darkness Ignorance and matter.

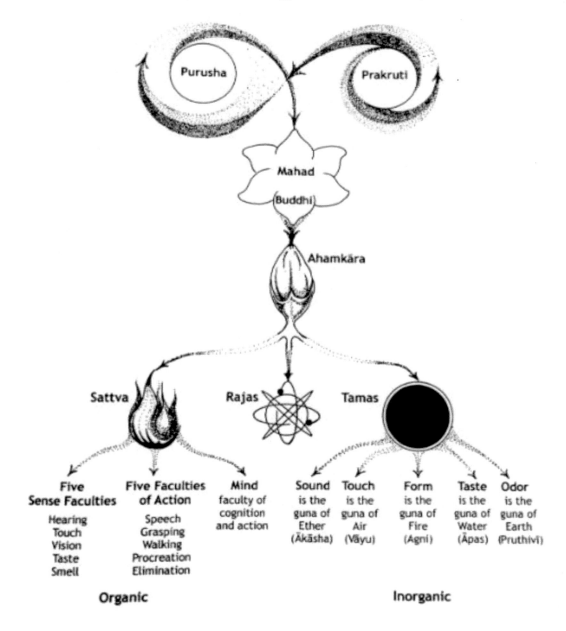

The wealth of knowledge is the precious wealth of all.
Image Taken from: Textbook of Ayurveda, Vol.1: Fundamental Principles of Ayurveda 1st Edition by Dr. Vasant Lad

Function of the respiratory system:

a) Warm, filter, and humidify air
b) Exchange oxygen for carbon dioxide

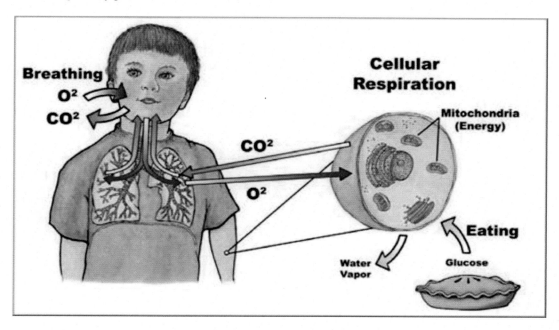

Given an optimal diet and healthy body, up to **70% of the body's metabolic waste is eliminated through the respiratory system**.

- 3% through defecation
- 8% through urination
- 19% through perspiration

The path of respiration starts with:

nose » palate » pharynx » larynx » trachea » bronchi » bronchioles » alveoli

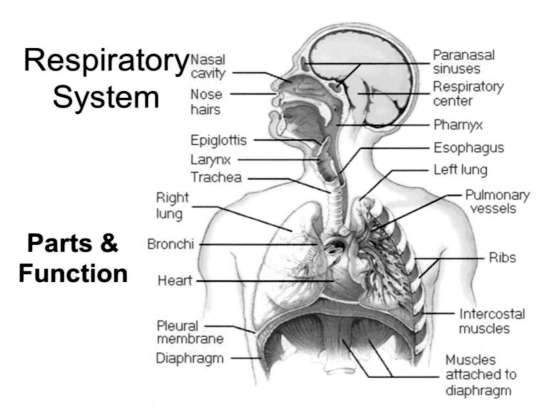

Respiratory System

Parts & Function

Nasal cavity

Nose hairs

Epiglottis

Larynx

Trachea

Right lung

Bronchi

Heart

Pleural membrane

Diaphragm

Paranasal sinuses

Respiratory center

Pharnyx

Esophagus

Left lung

Pulmonary vessels

Ribs

Intercostal muscles

Muscles attached to diaphragm

The lungs consist of:

   a) Bronchioles
   b) Alveoli
   c) Blood vessels
   d) Lymph vessels
   e) Air
   f) Spongy, elastic tissue

NOTE: The lungs do not expand on their own!

The primary muscle of inspiration is the diaphragm. The diaphragm is:

   a) sheath of muscle and tendon that divides the thorax from the abdomen
   b) Attaches to the lower ribs and lumbar vertebrae
   c) Contracting downward on inhalation and relaxing upward on exhalation

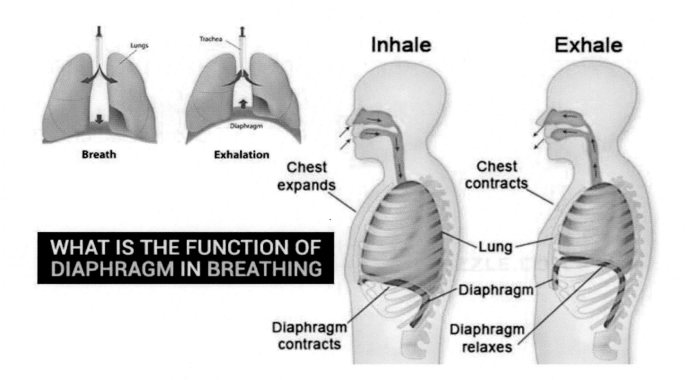

PRANAYAMA

Pranayama removes the veil covering the light of knowledge and heralds the dawn of wisdom. - Yoga Sutras of Patanjali 2:52

Prana *"vital energy, life force"* + ayama *"extension, expansion, freedom"*

During quiet breathing:

- Diaphragm moves up and down approximately 1-2 cm and the inter costal muscles expand the rib cage
- Approximately 500 ml of air is moved in and out

Inter "between" + costal "ribs"

During deep yogic breathing:

- Diaphragm can move as much as 10 cm and additional muscles become involved
- Approximately 3-4 quarts of air is moved in and out.

The complete breath: **∧ oxygen levels in the blood ∨ carbon dioxide**

- Muscles used are:
  a) Abdominal muscles
  b) Sternocleidomastoid and scalene
  c) Back muscles
  d) Transversus abdominus

Pranayama expands and heightens what is already present in the mind

Just as a lion, an elephant, or a tiger is tamed gradually, so should the life force be controlled, else it will kill the practitioner.

- **Hatha Yoga Pradipika –**

Pranayama develops a finer awareness of energy.

- Average person breaths 18 breaths per minute (**6+6+6**)
- Indoor office worker breathes approximately 3,000 gallons of air each day, absorbing 150 gallons of oxygen.
- A sneeze travels at 100 mph.
- Each lung weighs about one pound and contains 250,000 bronchioles and hundreds of millions of alveoli, tiny air sacs.
- The air we inhale is approximately 20% oxygen and we exhale approximately 16% oxygen.

NERVOUS SYSTEM

Neurons:

- are specialized cells that allow us to sense, move, think, and emote
- in the brain alone, there are an estimated 100 billion neurons (nerve cells)

The nervous system is divided into two parts:

- the central nervous system (includes the brain and the spinal cord)
- the peripheral nervous system (includes the 12 pairs of cranial nerves and 31 pairs of spinal nerves)

a) these nerves inform the brain about the external environment through touch, pressure, pain, joint position, muscle tension, chemical concentration, light, or other stimuli

b) the motor nerves carry movement command impulses from the central nervous system to the muscles

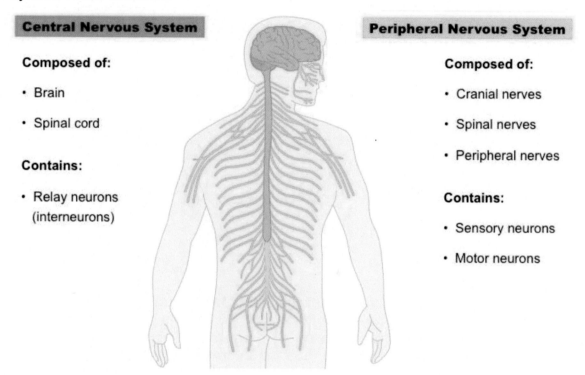

Central Nervous System

Composed of:

- Brain

- Spinal cord

Contains:

- Relay neurons (interneurons)

Peripheral Nervous System

Composed of:

- Cranial nerves

- Spinal nerves

- Peripheral nerves

Contains:

- Sensory neurons

- Motor neurons

Divisions of the Autonomic System

- autonomic nervous system is part of the peripheral nervous system
- is divided into the sympathetic and parasympathetic nervous system
- some scientists add an additional division known as the enteric nervous system (brain-gut); scientists are increasingly recognizing the "brain-gut connection."
- when the sympathetic nervous system is stimulated, we experience "fight or flight"
  a) the heart pounds
  b) blood pressure rises
  c) shallow and quick breathing
  d) body takes energy from the digestive, reproductive, and immune systems, slowing them down to maintenance levels
  e) hyper people exhaust the adrenal glands while the digestive and immune systems remain sluggish
  f) endorphins (neuro-transmitters) are compromised

- parasympathetic nerves:
  a) increase peristalsis (the smooth muscle movement of digestion)

Autonomic Nervous System
Sympathetic - "Fight or Flight"

Parasympathetic - "Rest and Digest"

Nerves serve as vessels in the body. Impulses from the brain travel through these vessels to give a 'command' to the appropriate organ to perform its particular function. When these pathways are hindered or the area of the brain responsible for relaying the message is compromised, the organ is no longer at ease, but rather 'dis-eased'. For example, a person may have eyes, but if the brain isn't able to relay the message to the eyes to take in light and focus, the individual may experience either impaired vision or blindness.

NOTE: The medical term for *'vessel'* is *angio-* from the Latinized Greek root *'angeion'*. This is very similar to the Greek *'angelos'* from which the English word *'angel'* is coined. Angelos means *'messenger'*. For illustrative purposes, let's imagine that the angelic beings are represented by the nervous system and that God is represented by the brain. Just as the body will be compromised and suffer imbalances if the *'message'* isn't properly communicated from the source, so does humanity experience the same fate if there's no synchronicity between the Source (Creator) and Man (creation).

Trees give fruits to assist others. Rivers flow to help others. Cows produce milk to feed others. In the same way our own human body should also be employed for the welfare of others.

Chapter 5: Yoga And The Endocrine System

The endocrine glands secrete hormones within (endo) the body.

Hormones (Gk-*"to urge on"*) are tiny yet powerful messengers that:

- signal and regulate growth
- reproduction
- metabolism
- other human functions

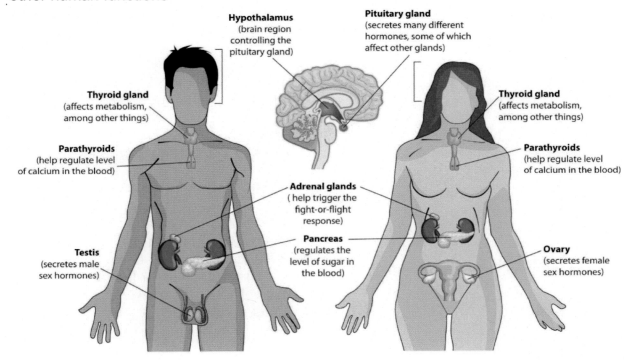

It has been said by one yoga teacher that, *"Your endocrine system is the medicine chest of the body — and yoga opens up the cabinet door."*

Another yoga teacher points out that *"hormones are the physical aspects of the chakras."*

Powers of accomplished yogis seem to indicate an ability to control the body's functions on a molecular level.

Yoga practice can stimulate and maintain the health of the endocrine system.

Ex. The postures physically stimulate the glands through stretching and squeezing them. Also, chanting stimulates through vibration and resonance, while mudras (hand gestures) and dharana (concentration) stimulate the energy body.

Practices Associated with the Endocrine System

Endocrine Gland	Yogasana, Mudra, etc.
Pituitary	Inversions (particularly the headstand) Khecari mudra (placing tongue in the nasal cavity) Brahmari pranayama (humming breath)
Pineal	Inversions (particularly the shoulder stand) Practice done in sunlight or moon light
Thyroid/Parathyroid	Sarvangasana (shoulder stand), matsyasana (fish), and other postures that flex and extend the neck area; chin lock
Thymus	Salabhasana (locust); Anjali mudra
Adrenals	Backbends (stimulate function) Forward bends (calms function) Rapid breathing (stimulates) Slow, deep breathing (calms)
Pancreas	Twisting poses Bow
Sex Organs	Mula bandha
Entire System	Surya namaskara

DINACHARYA- daily routine (ritual)
- Necessary to bring radical change in body, mind, and consciousness
- Regularizes one's biological clock
- Aids digestion, absorption, and assimilation
- Generates self-esteem, discipline, peace, happiness and longevity
- When practicing, feel that you are honoring yourself, body, and God

1) Wake up early in the morning
   - Preferably before "sunrise"; sattvic (loving) qualities are present at this time
     a) Vata people (6am)

    b) Pitta people (5:30am)
    c) Kapha people (4:30am)

- Cleanse aura
    a) Look at hands for a few moments
    b) Move them over your face and chest
    c) Waist

2) Say a prayer/affirmation before leaving bed

Examples:

"Dear God, you are inside of me, within my very breath, within each bird, within each mighty mountain. Your sweet touch reaches everything and I am well protected."

"Thank you, God, for this beautiful day

before me. May joy, love,
peace and compassion
be part of my life and all
those around me on this
day. I am healing, and I
am healed."

With the right hand:

- Touch the ground
- Touch the forehead with great
love and respect for Mother Earth

Kemetyu (Ancient

Egyptian) performing Sen-Ta.

3) Clean the face, mouth and eyes
- a) Face and mouth with cold water
- b) Eyes with cool water
- • Gently massage eyelids

- • Blink seven times and rotate eyes in all directions

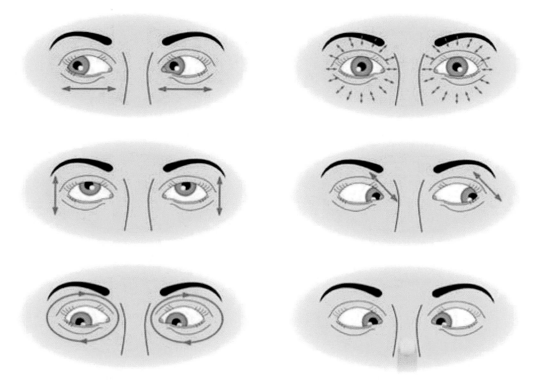

- • Dry face with a clean towel

4) Drink water in the morning
- a) Room temperature (preferably from a pure copper cup filled the previous night)

- This washes the GI tract, flushes kidney, and stimulates peristalsis
- Not a good idea to start the morning with caffeine (coffee or tea). THIS DRAINS THE KIDNEYS OF ENERGY!!! Also, stresses adrenals, causes constipation , and is habit forming.

5) Evacuation
   a) Sit, or better, squat on toilet and have a bowel movement
      - Improper digestion of previous night's meal can prevent this
      - Water followed by sitting on the toilet at a set time each day helps regulate bowel movements
      - Alternate nostril breathing may also help

AumSahaNaavavatu
Saha Nau Bhunaktu
SahaVeeryamKaravaavahai
TejasvinaaVadheetamatsu
MaaVidvishaaVahai ||
ShantihShantihShantih ||

"Let us protect each other. Let us eat together. Let us work together. Let us study together to be bright and successful. Let us not hate each other. Aum Peace, Peace, Peace."

Chapter 6: Food Combining

Poor food combining = gas + indigestion

Ayurveda teaches:
- understanding the individual is key to finding a truly balanced diet
- gastric fire (Agni) in the stomach and digestive tract is the main gate through which nutrients enter the tissues and then pass along to individual cells to maintain the life functions
- every food has its own taste (rasa)
- every food has a heating or cooling energy (virya)
- every food has a post-digestive effect (vipaka)
- every food has an unexplained effect (prabhava)

When two or more foods having different taste, energy and post digestive effect are combined:
- Agni can become overloaded
- inhibition of the enzyme system
- produces toxins
- produce indigestion, fermentation, putrefaction, and gas formation

If prolonged can lead to toxemia and disease.

> Ex. Bananas + milk = Diminished Agni
> Change intestinal flora
> Produces toxins
> Sinus congestion
> Cold, cough and allergies

If these same foods were eaten separately, they may:
- stimulate Agni
- be digested more quickly
- and even help to burn ama

Incompatible food combinations also cause confusion of the cells leading to many different diseases.

Tips to Aid Digestion

- Eat ½ tsp fresh grated ginger with a pinch of rock salt before each meal to stimulate Agni
- Salt also aids in digestion and helps retain water
- Alkalis help digestion and regulate digestive fire
- Ghee stimulates agni and improves digestion

- Small sips of warm water during each meal will aid digestion and absorption of food. Do not drink iced water as it slows agni and digestion. ICED WATER SHOCKS THE SYSTEM!
- Proper chewing is essential to good digestion. It ensures that the food gets thoroughly mixed with saliva.
- A cup of lassi at the end of a meal also aids the digestive process. Make by blending ¼ cup yogurt with 2 pinches of ginger and cumin powder in 1 cup water.
- Ideally, one should fill the stomach 1/3 food, 1/3 liquid and 1/3 empty.

Keep Food Combinations Simple

- Anything that aggravates doshas without expelling them is considered a bad food combination.
- Generally, Vatta has the most difficulty with poor food combinations because they do not have enough liquids to adequately break them down.
- Proper food combining is important for anyone with:
  a) A weakness
  b) Those recovering from illness, or
  c) Those wishing to cleanse and/or rejuvenate their bodies

- One pot meals (soups with a few simple ingredients) are generally easiest to digest.

Reduce the Enzymes You Need to Digest

Every ingredient requires separate enzymes from the gut.

Simple food combinations

Simple food combinations = Better focus from the body on each ingredient

  a) Eat no more than three main ingredients per meal
  b) Avoid mixing animal with vegetable proteins such as beans
  c) Eat proteins with leafy greens or rice only
  d) Avoid eating fruits within two hours of a meal. This forms a sour wine in the stomach.
  e) Avoid eating dairy (including cheese) within two hours of a meal. Milk curdles in the stomach if mixed with other foods.

Intestinal Health

Foods easiest to digest should be eaten first, and the hardest last.

Ex. Eat rice before lentils, steamed veggies before nuts.

The gut holds on to foods until all the nutrients have been extracted.

- Food that is easy to digest will ferment if not processed

Avoid proteins with foods that suppress stomach acid

Fatty and acidic foods reduces gastric acid secretions, specifically inhibiting protein digestion. For this reason, avoid mixing lemons with meats, oranges or nuts.
Meat is often fatty. Therefore, it should be eaten with bitters to counteract the digestion lulling properties of fats.

Cooking and Bad Food Combining

-   The effects of bad food combing decrease when foods are cooked together because their qualities blend together; i.e. soup.
-   Carefully chewing poor food combinations may help in situations where bad food combining is inevitable (restaurants).
-   Avoid:
    a) Combining raw foods with cooked foods
    b) Fresh foods with leftovers

Common Bad Food Combinations To Avoid

-   **Sandwich-** generally combines wheat mixed with meat, raw food (lettuce with cooked food (meat), and fermented food (cheese, sour cream, etc.)
-   **Cheeseburger-** made with meat, wheat and dairy. Each of these ingredients are difficult to digest separately. Together they confuse the stomach.
-   **Yogurt with fruit**
-   **Burritos-** often contains vegetable with animal proteins (beans and meat). Mixes meats with dairy (sour cream and cheese). Too many ingredients in general and mixes raw tomatoes with cooked food.
-   **Pizza-** mixes wheat with cheese and tomatoes
-   **Apples with peanut butter-** beans take a long time to digest. As the body churns away at the bean, the bacteria churn away at the fruit.
-   **Salad with tomatoes, cucumbers and raw mushrooms-** contains combination of raw foods of different energetics.

Sugar

-   Sucrose
-   Fructose
-   Maltose
-   Pure cane sugar
-   High fructose corn syrup
-   Dextrose
-   Glucose
-   Lactose
-   Corn syrup
-   Honey
-   Barley
-   Malt syrup

- Corn starch
- Turbinado
- Molasses
- Florida Crystals
- Artificial sweeteners
- Anything with *"-ose"* suffix

Sugar Facts

- Has NO nutritional value! It is DEPLETING!
- 1 tsp sugar depresses the immune system for approximately 5 HRS. There are 12 tsp sugar in one can of soda. **(12 tsp x 5 hrs = 60 hrs immune depressions!)**
- Acid forming
- Feeds tumors and cancer
- Toxic at high doses (1/2 tsp/day)
- **High fructose corn syrup and fructose are metabolized by the liver;** other sugars are metabolized by the intestinal mucosa
- 75% of U.S. health-care dollars are spent on diet-related diseases. **Nature made sugar hard to get, man made it easy!**
- From an evolutionary perspective, sugar in the form of fruit was available only a few months of the year, at harvest time.
- Honey was guarded by bees and therefore was a treat, not a dietary staple.

Al Qur'an 16:68-69

"And your Lord revealed to the bee saying: Make hives in the mountains and in the trees and in what they build: (68) Then eat of all the fruits and walk in the ways of your Lord submissively. <u>There comes forth from within it a beverage of many colors, in which there is healing for men;</u> most surely there is a sign in this for a people who reflect. (69)"

- Feeds bacterial yeast overgrowth- Candida
- People with acne don't metabolize sugar well
- Average American eats 100 lbs. of sugar per year/40 lbs. of fake sugar.
- 150 years ago average American consumed 1-2 lbs
- Dextrose- boiled cornstarch with acid
- At night can cause insomnia and night sweats
- Causes:
    a) Weight gain
    b) Aging
    c) Age spots
    d) Fatigue
    e) Depression
    f) Yeast infections
    g) Skin problems
    h) Increased pain
    i) Inflammation

j) Learning disabilities
k) Mood disorders
l) Anxiety
m) Bone loss
n) Uric acid production
o) Increased carbohydrate and alcohol addiction
p) Blood sugar imbalances (diabetes)
q) Adrenal fatigue
r) Tooth decay
s) Interrupts collagen production
t) arthritis

The body metabolizes sugar in the following ways:

- When we consume too much glucose, the pancreas releases insulin to stabilize the glucose and sends some of the excess glucose into the cells. In active individuals the glucose will be converted into energy. If it doesn't get used, the body stores it as triglycerides.
- A dangerous cycle is repeated when glucose levels spike and fall. This depletes the body and leaves it susceptible to chronic health conditions.
- Sugar temporarily increases dopamine
- Sugar addiction can physiological much like that of heroin, cocaine, and nicotine addictions. The behavior of "sugar addicts" are often typical of those found in alcoholics
- Sugar addiction is often a precursor to binge eating

CONSUMER BEWARE!

- By law, the FDA only requires that sucrose (table sugar) has to be mentioned on labels.
- So-called "balanced carbohydrate sources" are hidden sugars.
- Tobacco is *"cured"* in sugar!

THE SOLUTION…

- Stop cold turkey! Abstain from sugar for three to four weeks to allow your brain to reset.
- Eat a more diverse diet to minimize the withdrawal caused by the detoxification process. This should be done steadily and over a prolonged period of time.
- Stay hydrated! Water is best!
- Include a protein with each meal and healthy fats.
- Brush your teeth after meals and drink herbal tea. If possible, **avoid toothpastes with fluoride as this is actually a poison (fluoride contains arsenic and is a known carcinogen)**. Instead, use toothpaste that contains Neem.
- Exercise! Release glucose through perspiration.
- Make sure your glucose levels are balanced:
  a) Never allow yourself to get hungry.
  b) Always eat some form of protein for breakfast.

c) Have a protein snack throughout the day.
d) Think three meals ahead at all times.
e) Avoid high glycemic foods (white bread, white flour, white rice, etc.). Look for three or more grams of fiber.

- Be aware of any food allergies (parasites) that could trigger cravings.
- Adequate sleep curtails cravings.
- Engage in stress management (e.g., meditation)

Medicinal teas

SPICES

1) Asafoetida good for:
   - Bloating
   - Painful menstruation
   - Asthma
   - Arthritis

   - A pinch with warm sesame oil is massaged onto a colicky baby's stomach for rapid relief
   - A pinch to savory dishes imbues it with a rich oniony flavor whilst quieting uncomfortable after-dinner rumblings

2) Cardamom:

   Cardamom + deserts = sweet breath/clean airways

Cardamom + curry/deserts/dals = expelled mucus and reduced gassy indigestion

Cardamom + ginger = Stimulated appetite/respiratory system
Decreased nausea/coughs

Cardamom + coffee = protected adrenals

5 bruised cardamom pods
2 cinnamon sticks
2 peppercorns
4 ginger root slices
2 basil leaves

3) Cinnamon good for:
   - Warming winter dishes
   - Stimulating circulation
   - Warm backache
   - Halt hiccups

Pinch of cinnamon + ¼ cup apple cider vinegar = settled stomach

4) Cloves good for:
   - Sore throat
   - Stimulating taste buds
   - Coughs **(Pinch of clove + 1 tsp honey; 3x daily)**, or, inhale steam of **seven cloves + five cups of boiled water**
   - Toothache (few drops of clove oil on a cotton ball placed over the tooth)
   - Kills parasites

5) Coriander (cilantro) contains:

   - Natural antihistamine
   - Vitamin C
   - Bioflavonoid (decreases allergic reactions such as hay fever)
   - Eliminates heavy metal buildup from the body

For cooking:
   - Grind whole seeds into a powder
   - Lightly fry and add to dishes

Fresh leaves:
   - Store by cutting off roots
   - Drain moisture
   - Keep in a sealed plastic bag
   - Use as a garnish of stir-fry, rice, or salad
   - Chutney is a delicious accompaniment to any vegetable dish

6) Cumin (cum-an'-get-it!) relieves:

- Gas
- Menstrual pain
- Diarrhea

1 tsp cumin seeds + 1 tsp fennel seeds + ¼ tsp ground ginger + ½ tsp rock vinegar + pinch of rock salt = boosts digestion

*chew ½ tsp after meals

Tea: ½ tsp seeds + 2 cups boiling water (reduced to one cup) + peppermint tea =

relief from colicky

7) Curry leaves good for:

- Soothing upset stomach
- Cooling burning pain of ulcers
- Ease diarrhea

FRESH LEAVES ARE BEST!

8) Fenugreek:

- Increases breast milk
- Reduces menstrual pain and stomach cramps
- Hypoglycemic
- Lymphatic and lung decongestant (such as smoker's cough)
  1 tsp fenugreek seeds + 2 cups boiling water (boiled down to one cup); strain and drink **3x daily**

AVOID DURING PREGNANCY! STIMULATES UTERINE CONTRACTIONS!

1 tsp powder + 1 liter cooked rice water = stimulated hair growth (rinse through hair)

9) Ginger (known in India as Viswabeshaj; "universal medicine")

Effective remedy for:

- Poor circulation
- Coughs
- Colds
- Flu
- Poor digestion and nausea
- Morning and motion sickness

Either chew the root or enjoy as a tea

10) Nutmeg effective for:

- Diarrhea and malabsorption
- Crohn's disease sufferers

¼ tsp ground nutmeg + 1 tsp cumin seeds + 3 curry leaves + boiled, soupy rice for breakfast = stop the runs

¼ tsp freshly grated nutmeg + ½ cup warm milk = sound sleep

NUTMEG HAS HALLUCINOGENIC PROPERTIES, ONLY SMALL QUANTITIES SHOULD BE USED!

11) Saffron:

Fabulous female tonic that:

- Boosts libido
- Increases milk flow
- Reduces menstrual pain
- Boosts fertility

- Adulterates with calendula or chrysanthemum petals due to its high cost
- To maximize its color, aroma and flavor:
  - Sit threads in a small quantity of water or milk for 20 minutes
  - Add dish when only five minutes remain in cooking it

Males:

- Male seminal incontinence
- Sexual exhaustion

12) Turmeric (queen of the kitchen; reigning healer among kitchen spices)

- Known in India askrimighna meaning "germ killer"
- As antiseptic wash:
  - Gives on a golden aura; hence its use for bridal baths and countering skin infections or blemishes
  - Combats throat infections (**1/2 tsp turmeric + 2 cloves + 1 cup boiled water; sit for five minutes, strain + 1 drop teat tree oil + 1 cup of rock or seas salt; gargle 3x daily**)
- Face mask:
  1 part turmeric + 1 part sandalwood powder + 12 parts chickpea flour + 1 tbs buttermilk
  - Apply to the face and wash off with cold water after 10 minutes

- To preserve, keep in a dark container in a cool cupboard

Ayurvedic Herbs

1) ADRAK

English name: Ginger

Latin Name: officinale

Dose: ginger juice, arshoghna, deepaniya, shoolaprashaman (Painkiller), trushnanigraham,
        pippalyadi, trikatu, panchakola, shadushan.

Properties:

Guna:laghu, Singha (ginger is ruksha, tiksha, guru)

Veeraya: Ushna

Vipak: Madhur

Rasa: Katu

Srotogamitva:

Dosha: KaphaVataghna

Dhatu: Rasa

Mala: Purisha

Organ: Heart, internal and external routes. Its reducing swelling.

CNS: Stimulate nerves, relives pain, impulse transmission, Vata disorders.

Digestive: carminative, appetizer, vkp, RA, antispasmodic, indigestion, nausea.

Circulatory: anti-inflammatory, cardiac debility, pain edema, urticaria.

Respiratory: Kaphaghna, anti-asthmatics, pharyngitis, bronchitis.

Reproductive: Due to Madhur Vipak aphrodisiac.

Satmikaran: general debility, post partum debility, reduces swelling, agni(Vardhan and kledpachak) and Vata.

2) TULASI:

English Name: Ocimum sanctum linn.

Latin Name: Ocimum derived from Greek work okimon. used for religious purpose.

Gana:surasadi.

Properties:

Guna: laghu,ruksha.

Rasa:katu,tikta.

Veeraya:ushna.

Vipak:katu.

Srotogamitva:

Dosha: Pittavardhak, KaphaVatashamak

Dhatu: Rakta(skin disorders), fat metabolism

Mala: Mutra(dysuria), Diaphoretic, mala.

Organ: Heart,respiratory system.

Digestive: appetizer, laxative and anthelmintic, it is used in anorexia,emesis, abdominal pain and helminthiasis. Tulsi leaves should be chewed in pyorrhea.

Circulatary: cardiac stimulant, blood purifier and anti-inflammatory. Used in cardiac debility,

Vata Kaphadi orders of blood and inflammations.

Respiratory:they act as expectorant and alleviate the symptoms like cough induces by kapgha, dyspnoea and fever.

Satmikaran: seed is tonic. Kheer prepared from the seed should be in debility due to Pittadosha.

3) AJMODA

English name: Carumroxburghianumbeith

Latin Name: Carumroxburghianum, carum as well as seed are edible.

Gana:schoolaprashaman, deepaniya, pippalyadi.

Properties:

Guna:laghu,ruksh,tikshna.

Veeraya:ushna(tikshna).

Vipak:katu.

Rasa:katu,tikta.

Srotogamitva:

Dosha: Reduces Kapha and Vata.

Dhatu:shukra(aphrodisiac).

Mala:purisha(anti-helminthic).

Organ:basti(bladder), netra(eyes),hridya(heart), garbhashay(uterus).

CNS: the decoction of roots nourishes brain and gives strength to nerve. It is contraindicted inepilepsy.

Digestive: carminative, appetizer, analgesic and anthelmintic. It is used is emesis, loss of appetite, hiccups, flatulence, stomachache and helminthiasis.

Circulatary: it acts as cardiac stimulant in cardiac disorders.

Respiratory:used in cough asthma, hiccough in the form of churna(powder)and also form in smoke(dhoomapan).

Satmikaran: it is bitter and nutrient. Used in general debility.

4) KUMARI

English Name: Indian Aloe

Latin Name: Aloe

Properties:

Guna:snigdha, pichchil;

Rasa; bitter, sweet;

Vipak: Katu.

Veeray:sheeta.

Prabhav:bhedan.

Kala bol:laghu, ruksha, tishna and ushna.

Srotogamitva:

Dosha: Vata reducing, cough reducing, Pittasarak.

Dhatu:rasayani, mansa(bruhanil),shukra(vrushya), rakta(jaundice), rasa.

Mala:purisha (bhedak), artavajanak.

Organ: eyes, uterus.

Prabhav: has antidotal properties. poultice-anti-inflammatory parts. Swollen, painful, enlarged spleen(kumari+turmeric)

Digestive: Deepan, pachan, bhedam and uttejak, virechaka, kruminghna juice of kumari in loss of appetite, tumor, liver, spleen, enlargement, abdominal colic, laxative, antiflatulent.

Cardiovascular:yakritgami, raktavahasrotogami purification of blood and affections of liver, splenomegaly kumari+haridra.

Satmikaran: poultice-anti-inflammatory parts.Swollen, painful, enlarged spleen(kumari+turmaric)

5) ERAND

English name: Castor plant

Latin Name: Ricinus communis

Gana: Bhendiya, swedopag, angamardaprashaman, madhurskandha, vidarigandhadi, adhobhagahar, Vatasanshaman.

Properties:

Guna: guru, snigdha, tikshna, sukshma;

Rasa: Madhur, katu, Kashaya.

Vipak: Madhur.

Veerya:ushna.

Prabhav: purgative.

Srotogamitva:

Dosha: Vata-Kapha-Pitta.

Dhatu: shukraroot(aphrodisiac)

Rasa: beneficial to skin rakta(complexion), raktaprakopan, vayasthapan(rasayan), majja(promotes intellect), hepatosplemomegaly, lactogenic.

Mala: oil-purisha(purgative), shodhanand helminthiasis.

Organ: lower half of body (bladder pain head ache), joints(amVata).

CNS: decreasing Vata, rejuvenating, analgesic, medhya, relieving body ache. Used for diseases such as hemiplegia, fecial palsy, sciatica, tremors as well as headache and body ache.

Digestive: it is deepan being ushnaveerya ,bhedan by tikshnaguna,athelminticbysnigdha. Oil taken at breakfast cures chronic constipation. Used in ascites, abdominal colic, tumors, hepatosplenomegaly and piles.

Circulatary: it is useful in cardiac pain as well as in oedema.

Respiratory: it is Kaphaghna by its ushna and tikshna property and useful in bronchitis and asthma with predominanceof Kapha.

Satmikaran: balya and anti-aging, antidode

Ayurvedic Nutritious Food Recipes
Cilantro (pesto)Chutney
(Replace with Parsley/Basil)

Ingredients:

½ Cup	Cilantro, Leaves, Fresh Chopped
½ Cup	Coconut, Fresh Grated or Dried
½ Tsp	Ginger, Fresh Grated
½ Tsp	Cumin, Whole Seeds

1 Tsp	Lime Juice, Fresh
2 cloves	Garlic (For Garlic Lovers)
¼ Tsp	Salt (Less or more as per your taste)
	Water- Just Enough to Mix Together

Preparations:

First of all separate the stem and leaves of cilantro. Wash cilantro leaves thoroughly, then chop cilantro removing thick stems. Add cilantro leaves coconut, grated ginger, cumin seeds, lime juice, and salt into blender. Blend together at high speed until it is thoroughly until it is mixed together very well (it should be like a fine paste). You may need to add a small amount of water. This chutney can be eaten as an appetizer with other foods.

Tip-I use whole cilantro leaves and stems all together in the dish. Choice is always yours.

Add fistful almonds or walnuts in the same process in the blender depending upon your your likes and dislikes.

Can eat as a spread or pesto or garnish of sautéed vegetables etc.

Benefits:

Source of easy Antioxidant.

One of the best chutney to eat in summer season.

Calms the immune system and helps for removing excess heat from body .It softens stool , it's diuretic healthful for kidneys and a blood cleanser.

Balances all three doshas. Cilantro has cooling properties, it reduces the Pitta dosha. Both Ginger and Cumin Stimulate and Aid in Digestion.

Yellow Mung Dal Soup

(Replace with Red Lentil)

Ingredients:

1 Cup	Yellow Split Mung Dal
	(with or without skin)
6 Cups	Water
2 Tbs	Ghee (Clarified Butter)
½ Tsp	Black Mustard Seed

1 Tsp	Cumin Seeds, Whole
1 Pinch	Hing(Asafoetida)
1 Tsp	Turmeric powder
2 Tbs	Chopped Fresh Cilantro Leaves
½ Tsp	Salt (Rock Salt is Best)
½ Tsp	Coriander Seeds, Ground
½ Tsp	Cumin Seeds, Ground
½ Tsp	Jaggery or Brown crystal sugar
	(Optional just for additional taste)
¼ Tsp	Lime juice

Preparations:

Wash the mung dal until the water runs clear. Heat pot on medium heat, add water and dal. Cook for 30 minutes. Stir occasionally to prevent burning. Then in sauce pan at medium heat add ghee. When it is liquid you can add spices , turmeric powder and salt (add salt to taste). Then add spicy ghee mix to soup. Add jaggery here at this moment which is optional. Add lime juice in the pan . Before serving garnish with freshly chopped leaves.

Can eat alone or with rice .

Benefits:

Mung is easy to digest .It is one of the best Saatvic food . It is nourishing the tissues so automatically nourishing Immune system. It has calming and grounding effects on Mind And Body.

This dish reduces both Kapha and Vatadoshas. With the spices it reduces the Pitta dosha. It is very easy to digest.

Lime Rice

(One of the type of Healthy Rice)

Ingredients:

2 Cup	White Basmati Rice
4Cups	Water
2 Tbs	Chickpea/Urad Dal or Mung Dal
1 Tsp	Mustard Seeds
1 Tsp.	Cumin seeds
1Tsp	Turmeric Powder
2Tbs	Ground Coconut
2	Pinch of Hing
2Tsp	Whole Cumin Seeds
3Tsp	Fresh Lime Juice (or More to Taste)
4Tbs	Ghee
2Tsp	Salt

Preparations:

Cooking rice and dal with water for 10 to 12 minutes. Saute spices (except for lime juice and salt) in melted ghee. Then mix rice and sauteed spice mix together (along with lime juice). Add salt and lime juice before serving you can add cilantro and grated coconut to make the dish more colorful.

Benefits:

It Strengthens the Agni which will help to improve digestion so will help to Immune system in the future .alances all three doshas. Both ginger and cumin stimulates and aid in digestion.

Yogi Ayur Tea

Ingredients:

10 oz	Water
1 Tsp	Tulsi/Holy Basil Powder
3	Cloves
4	Green Cardamon Pods
4	Whole Peppercorns
½	Stick of Cinnamon
1	Slice Ginger Root
¼ Tsp	Black Tea
½ Cup Milk	
1 Tsp	Lemon Grass optional

Preparation:

Boil spices for 10-15 minutes. Add black tea and steep for 2 minutes. Add milk, then reheat to boiling point. Remove immediately from stove and strain. Add honey or natural sugar to taste only if needed.

Tip- Honey should not be added in hot liquids .

Can be added only at Luke warm or room temperature atmosphere.

To make more than 1 quart you can proportionally fewer species per cup. For 2 quarts:

20	Cardamon Pods
2	Peppercorns
15	Cloves
2 Tbs	Fennel seeds
1/8Tsp	Ajwain(caraway/carom seeds)
3	Cinnamon Sticks

1 Tbsp   Black Tea

Boil at least 30 minutes. Add 1 quart Milk.

Benefits:

Ajwain good for promoting digestion, relieves gases, bloating, improves constipation and weight loss, Black pepper is blood purifier. Cardamon is for the colon. Cardamon and black pepper together support brain cells. Cloves are for the nervous system. Cinnamon is for the bones. Ginger adds flavor, strengthens the nervous system and is good if you suffer from flu, cold or any physical illness. Milk aids i the assimilation of the spices and reduces any irritation to the colon and stomach. Fennel is a soothing spice which is extremely good for digestion and enhances the Agni. Fennel is a mouth freshener so in Indian culture people eats one tsp of fennel right after the meal consumption.

Essential Oils

What are essential oils?

Essential oils are compounds extracted from plants. The oils capture the plant's scent and essence. Unique aromatic compounds give each essential oil its characteristic essence.

Essential oils are obtained through distillation (via steam and/or <u>water</u>) or mechanical methods, such as cold pressing. Once the aromatic chemicals have been extracted, they are combined with a carrier oil to create a product that's ready for use. The way the oils are made is important, as essential oils obtained through chemical processes are not considered true essential oils.

Vibrational Frequency of Essential Oils

There is a subtle bio-energy that flows through all organic life. This lie-force goes by many names; prana, chi, ki, just to name a few. This energy is expressed as an electromagnetic vibrational frequency – *and pure essential oils have the highest frequencies of any measured natural substance.*

What is vibrational frequency?

Physics has demonstrated that nothing is truly at rest; **everything vibrates**. Every atom in the universe has a specific range of vibration and motion. Each motion has a frequency (the number of oscillations per second) that can be measured in Hertz. Every element in the Periodic Table has a specific vibratory frequency.

Most plants and animals use enzymes to break down molecular components during their life processes. Each of these enzymes has a unique crystalline form with a specific vibratory frequency. The vibrational frequency of an oil reflects the integrity of these elements and enzymes embodied within its life force and original intent. This contributes to an essential oil's potential therapeutic value.

During his work with plants, soil, and water in his agricultural projects, Bruce Tainio of Tainio Technology invented and built a machine called a BT3 Frequency Monitoring System. This device used a highly sensitive sensor to measure bio-electrical frequencies of plant nutrients and essential oils.

To summarize how it worked – As a Hertzian wave is generated and travels out from its source, it transfers energy to the objects it passes through. The frequency monitor's sensor measures the nano voltage of that wave, using the predominant frequency in the megahertz range, filtering out the lower and higher ranges. The BT3 measures the composite frequency of the vibratory emissions in electrical voltage – MHz – of the elements and enzymes remaining in the oils.

For example, here are the average frequencies of some of the therapeutic grade essential oils that have been measured:

Rose (Rosa damascene)	**320 MHz**
Lavender (Lavendula angustifolia)	**118 MHz**
Myrrh	**105 MHz**
Blue Chamomile	**105 MHz**
Juniper (Juniperusosteosperma)	**98 MHz**
Aloes/Sandalwood	**96 MHz**
Angelica	**85 MHz**
Peppermint	**78 MHz**
Galbanum	**56 MHz**
Basil	**52 MHz**

The measured frequencies of essential oils begin at 52 MHz, the frequency of basil oil, and go as high as 320 MHz — the frequency of rose oil. For comparison, dry herbs and foods have a frequency from 15 to 22 MHz, and fresh foods from 20 to 27 MHz. Processed and canned foods have no measurable frequency whatsoever.

Human Electrical Frequencies and Fields

Dr. Robert O. Becker, in his book *The Body Electric,* tells us that the human body has an electrical frequency, and also that much about a person's health can be determined by its frequency levels. In addition to his plant studies, Tainio developed a way to use his machine to measure human electrical vibrational frequency by taking readings on various points of the body and averaging those numbers together. His measurements indicate that the daytime frequency of a healthy human body vibrates in the range of **62 to 68 MHz**.

Intriguing as Tainio's research is, its foundation may have been laid in the early years of the 20th century by Dr. Royal R. Rife, M.D. (1888-1971). Dr. Rife conducted research with a machine he developed called a "frequency generator" that applies currents of specific frequencies to the body. He concluded that <u>**every disease has a specific frequency**</u>.

According to Dr. Rife every cell, tissue and organ has its own vibratory resonance. Working with his frequency generator, he found that specific frequencies would destroy a cancer cell or a virus. His research demonstrated that certain frequencies could prevent the development of disease, and that others would neutralize disease.

Bjorn Nordenstrom, a radiologist from Stockholm, Sweden, discovered in the early 1980s that, <u>by putting an electrode inside a tumor and running a milliamp of DC current through the electrode, he could dissolve a cancer tumor and stop its growth.</u> He also found that the human body had electropositive and electronegative energy fields.

Studies conducted in 1992 by Tainio Technology, as an independent division of Eastern State University in Cheny, Washington, reinforce the findings of these earlier researchers. Tainio and colleagues determined that when a person's frequency *drops below the optimum healthy range,* the immune system is compromised. Findings supported by this research indicate that:

Human cells start mutate below	**62MHz.**
Cold or the flu	**58 MHz**
Candida is present in the body	**55MHz.**
Epstein-Barr	**52 MHz**
Cancer	**42 MHz**
Death	**20 MHz.**

Effects of Outside Influences on Body Frequency

The study of frequencies raises an important question – how do the frequencies of substances found in our environment affect our personal frequency? Based on his studies, researcher Nikola Tesla said that, if we could eliminate certain outside frequencies that interfered in our bodies, we would have greater resistance toward disease.
Pathogens have a low frequency. Pollutants lower a healthy frequency. Processed and canned food having a frequency of zero can greatly diminish a person's own frequency. Even thoughts and feelings have a vibratory quality that forms a measurable frequency. A negative mental state can lower a person's frequency by 10-12 MHz.

Negative Thoughts	-12
Positive Thoughts	+10
Praying	+15
Smelling Coffee	- 8
Drinking Coffee	-14
Holding a Cigarette	-17
Smoking a Cigarette	-23

Likewise, a substance or influencing factor – such as thoughts, emotions, and frequency devices – in our internal and external environments can also serve to *raise* our frequencies. For example, a positive mental attitude, prayer or meditation can raise it by 10-15 MHz.

A substance with a higher frequency can raise a lower frequency due to the *principle of entrainment* – the tendency for two oscillating bodies to lock into phase so that they vibrate in harmony. This principle is key to understanding the effect essential oils can have on our personal electromagnetic frequency.

However, different types of frequencies can have a chaotic or a harmonizing effect on our own systems. When something vibrates at many dissonant frequencies, it produces "chaotic or incoherent frequencies." (David Stewart, *The Chemistry of Essential Oils Made Simple*).

For example, all of the electrical devices in your home emit electromagnetic vibrational frequencies that are incoherent and chaotic; i.e., lamps, television, radio, phone, microwave, etc. Their effect fractures the human electrical field.

By contrast, Dr. Rife's frequency generator and most naturally occurring substances – including essential oils – have coherent frequencies that resonate harmoniously with the electrical field of the human body.

The Healing Process and the Subtle Energy of Essential Oils

The human body vibrating within its normal vibratory range between 62 and 68 MHz is considered in *a state of health*. **But energy disturbances in the subtle bodies will actually precede the appearance of disease and illness in the physical body.**The normally harmonious coherent frequencies of the body easily go out of "tune" when a person experiences physical or emotional stress. **A blockage of the flow of life energy – characterized by inflammation, irritation and illness – can result.** When the human frequency range drops below the norm of 62 megahertz, this is when abnormal processes can begin to develop.

When disease and illness are present, they may manifest as chemical imbalances. But underlying this is an electromagnetic imbalance that has altered the specific vibrational frequencies of molecules, cells, tissues and organs within the body.

Properly "retuning" the body to its original frequency brings it into balance and restores its natural harmonic resonance – illness either doesn't manifest or is resolved.

Dr. Richard Gerber MD, author of *Vibrational Medicine,* tells us that one of the best ways we can change dysfunctional patterns in our energy bodies is to administer therapeutic doses of **"frequency-specific subtle energy in the form of vibrational medicines."**

And researcher Jim Oschman, PhD, who wrote *Energy Medicine,* refers to natural substances from the plant kingdom he calls *"energetic pharmacology"* (as distinguished from chemical pharmacology). **Therapeutic grade essential oils produce coherent frequencies that are naturally tuned to the health of our bodies. Pharmaceuticals and synthetic oils do not.**

The intention of this healing process is to provide the correct frequency that will bring the body back to a state of coherence, to a state of equilibrium. Terry Friedman, in his book, *Freedom Through Health* tells us that raising our vibrational frequency aids in **"restoring health to the body, clarity to the mind and attunement to the spirit."**

By applying an essential oil with a particular frequency to the human body – through the principle of entrainment – the oil's higher frequency will raise the vibratory quality of that individual. When several oils are blended together, each having a different MHz frequency, a frequency will emerge that may be higher or lower than the various components. The therapeutic properties create special vibrational remedies capable of healing or rebalancing the body/mind/soul/spirit.

And because each oil has a specific frequency, and our organs and body systems and the nutrients needed to maintain optimum health each have their specific frequencies, the oil's electrical affinity to these components of our bodies will enhance and support these organs and body systems, and will aid in the assimilation of nutrients.

Essential oils in the higher frequency ranges tend to influence the emotions. Essential oils in the lower frequencies have more effect on structural and physical changes, including cells, hormones, and bones as well as viruses, bacteria, and fungi.
Essential oils do not resonate with the toxins in our bodies. This incompatibility is what helps eliminate the toxins from our systems. Neither do they resonate with negative emotions. They can help dislodge forgotten traumas by surfacing them in our consciousness where we can deal with them and let them go.

Clinical research shows that essential oils have the highest frequency of any natural substance known to man, creating an environment in which disease, bacteria, virus, fungus, etc., cannot live. I believe that the chemistry and frequencies of essential oils have the ability to help man maintain the optimal frequency to the extent that disease cannot exist.

Gary Young of Young Living Essential Oils

The beauty of using therapeutic grade essential oils to restore coherent healthy vibrational frequencies to the body is that they are:

- Affordable
- Accessible
- Effective
- Versatile

Essential oils offer us a natural way to restore our body's healthy electromagnetic vibrational frequency. The elegance of their holism allows for easy functionality in our daily lives. Their constant subtle presence gently resonates with our body's electrical fields aiding and restoring harmonic health and well-being on all levels.

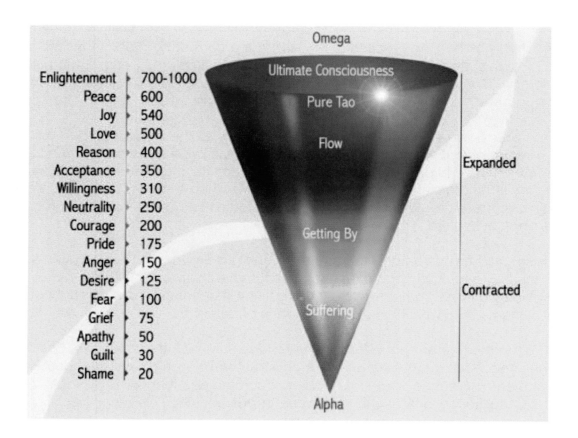

Mind – Body -Satva(Soul) Balance to enter in to the vital source of energy. ArunaPatki explores and explains in this book, demystifying their role in facilitating healing, balance, personal power, and everyday well-being. She offers meditations and visualizations, yoga postures, breathing exercises, and Ayurvedic dietary practices to learn about and work with the chakras. Positioned along the spinal axis, from the tailbone to the crown of the head, the seven main energy centers of the body are called chakras You may choose to follow the healing practices for seven days, devoting one day to each chakra; for seven weeks, focusing on each chakra for a week at a time; or at your own pace, spending as long as you need on each chakra. Whether you are experiencing an illness brought on by imbalance, feeling sluggish because of seasonal changes, or simply wishing to deepen your study of the subtle body, you will find healing and rejuvenation while discovering the power of these vibrant energy centers chakras.

AYURVEDA WINTER GROCERY LIST

VEGETABLES
Asparagus
Beets
Carrots
Green beans (cooked)
Okra
Peppers
Squash (all kinds)
Sweet potatoes
Turnips

PROTEIN
Beef
Chicken
Eggs
Lentils (brown/red)
Mung beans
Tofu
Turkey
Cheese (soft/hard)

SPICES
Black pepper
Cinnamon
Fennel
Garlic
Ginger
Nutmeg
Turmeric

OILS
Almond
Olive
Sesame

FRUITS
apples (cooked)
apricots
avocados
bananas
figs (fresh)
grapefruit
lemon/limes
mangoes
oranges

GRAINS
amaranth
oats (cooked)
rice (all)
wheat

DAIRY
buttermilk

cow's milk
ghee
yogurt

NUTS
almonds
cashews
pecans

TEA
cinnamon
ginger
tulsi

AYURVEDA SPRING GROCERY LIST

VEGETABLES
Arugula
Asparagus
Bell pepper
Broccoli
Brussel sprouts
Cabbage
Celery
Green beans
Kale
Spinach

FRUITS
All berries
Apples
Grapefruit
Lemons/limes
Pears

SPICES
Black pepper
Cayenne
Cinnamon
Coriander
Fennel
Ginger
Turmeric

NUTS
Pumpkin
Sunflower

PROTEIN
aduki beans
black beans
chicken
chickpeas
freshwater fish
lentils
mung beans
turkey

TEA
Cardamom
cinnamon
ginger
hibiscus
orange peel

OILS
Avocado
coconut
flax
hemp

GRAINS
barley
basmati rice
couscous

millet
quinoa

AYURVEDA SUMMER GROCERY LIST

VEGETABLES
Artichokes
Asparagus
Bell pepper
Broccoli
Celery
Cauliflower
Cucumber
Kale
Seaweed
Snow peas
Zucchini

PROTEIN
Adzuki beans
Chicken (white meat)
Chickpeas
Fava beans
Freshwater fish
Mung beans
Split pea

DAIRY
Ghee
Whole milk

GRAINS
Barley
Basmati rice

NUTS
Coconut
Sunflower

FRUITS
all berries
apples
apricots
cantaloupe
grapes
mangos
melons (all)
persimmons
plums
pineapple
pomegranate

SPICES
basil
chamomile
cilantro
coriander
fennel
parsley
turmeric

OILS
coconut
olive
sunflower

TEA
chicory
dandelion

hisbiscus
mint

AYURVEDA FALL GROCERY LIST

VEGETABLES
Avocados
Beets
Brussel sprouts
Carrots
Chilies
Okra
Onions
Pumpkins
Sweet potatoes

PROTEIN
Beef
Chicken
Eggs
Fish
Mung beans
Turkey
Tempeh

SPICES
Basil
Black pepper
Cardamom
Cinnamon
Fennel
Ginger
Turmeric

OILS
Almond
Olive
Sesame

FRUITS
apples (cooked)
bananas
dates
figs
grapefruit
grapes
lemons/limes
mangoes
oranges

GRAINS
oats
quinoa
rice (basmati & brown)
wheat

DAIRY
butter
cheese
cream
ghee
milk (warm)

NUTS
almonds
cashews
pistachio

TEA
chamomile
cinnamon
orange peel

Prakkrutih pansha bhutani graha loka swarastatha
Dishah kalashcha sarvesham sada kurvantu Mangalam ||

"May nature, composed of the: three qualities (SDat, Rajas, Tama); five elements (earth, water, fire, air, space); nine planets and fourteen worlds; seven notes of music with all their variations; ten directions and time (past, present, future), cause perpetual good to us."

Create your own routine with few of the Yoga Poses

Bitilasana/ Marjaiasana

Cow/ Cat Postures

Purpose: waking up the spine, bringing fluid to spine, hip joints and shoulder joints

Cues: come to hands and knees, align shoulders over wrists and hips over knees

Inhale: lift gaze, lift tail bone, heart forward, broaden chest (1. Bitilasana)

Exhale: press into hands, gaze toward naval, relax head and neck, round spine (2. Marjaisana)

Sequence: alternate between Bitilasana and Marjaisana following the rhythm of breath

Tadasana
Mountain Posture

Cues: spine tall, feet together (1.) or hip width apart (2.), press down into feet, lift kneecaps, draw low belly up and in, relax shoulders, soft gaze or eyes closed, arms at sides (1.) or hands press at heart (2.)

Sequence: (see Ardha Surya Namaskar, Surya Namaskar A, Surya Namaskar B)

UrdhvaHastasana
Upward Salute Posture

Cues: Stand in Tadasana

Inhale: reach arms over head, root down into feet, lengthen spine

Sequence: (see Ardha Surya Namaskar, Surya Namaskar A, Surya Namaskar B)

Uttanasana
Standing Forward Bend Posture

Cues: bend knees, fold upper body over legs, bring chest to rest on thighs, relax shoulders, head and neck, hold an elbow in each hand

Sequence: (see Ardha Surya Namaskar, Surya Namaskar A, Surya Namaskar B)

ArdhaUttanasana
Halfway Lift Posture

Cues: lift head and chest up, lengthen spine and neck, gaze toward floor, fingertips to shins, knees bent or legs straight

Sequence: (see Ardha Surya Namaskar, Surya Namaskar A, Surya Namaskar B)

Ardha Surya Namaskar
Half Sun Salutatio

Purpose: Connecting movements in body to breath, generate heat in body

Sequence: Begin in Tadasana(1)
Inhale reach arms overhead (2)
Exhale fold forward (3)
Inhale lift up halfway (4)
Exhale fold forward (5)
Inhale rise to stand, reach arms overhead (6)

Exhale hands to heart center (7)

Phalakasana
Plank Posture

Cues: shoulders over wrists, legs straight, press back through heels, lift belly, press into hands, shoulder blades press away from each other, gaze to top of mat

Sequence: (see Surya Namaskar A, Surya Namaskar B)

Chaturanga Dandasana
Four Limbed Staff Posture

Cues: from Phalakasana, lower knees, lower chest, elbows hug in, shoulder blades press toward each other

Sequence: (see Surya Namaskar A, Surya Namaskar B)

UrdhvaMukhaSvanasana(1)/ Bhujangasana(2)

Upward Facing Dog/ Cobra Postures

Cues: 1. Press into hands and tops of feet, lift knees and thighs up, shoulders down and back, lengthen neck, gaze forward or toward sky, heart forward,

      2. Press tops of feet and pubic bone down, lift heart, head and shoulders, hug elbows in, gaze foward

Sequence: (see Surya Namaskar A, Surya Namaskar B)

AdhoMukhaSvanasana
Downward Facing Dog Posture

Cues: lift tailbone, draw belly up and in, knees bent or legs straight, heels reach toward floor, spread fingers, press into hands, gaze toward naval

Sequence: (see Surya Namaskar A, Surya Namaskar B)

Surya Namaskar A
Sun Salutation A

Begin in Tadasana (1.)
Inhale UrdhvaHastasana (2.)
Exhale fold forward (3.)
Inhale to ArdhaUttanasana (4.)
Exhale step back to Phalakasana (5.)
Inhale.
Exhale lower to Chaturanga (6.)
Inhale to UrdhvaMukhaSvanasana or Bhujangasana (7.)
Exhale to AdhoMukhaSvanasana (8.)
Step to top of mat
Inhale to ArdhaUttanasana (9.)
Exhale to Uttanasana (10.)
Inhale to UrdhvaHastasana (11.)
Exhale Tadasana (12.)

Virabhadrasana I
Warrior I Posture

Bend the front knee, knee over ankle

Press into both feet

Reach arms over head, relax shoulders

Gaze forward or slightly up

Lift heart

Draw belly up and in

Utkatasana
Chair Posture

Feet together

Bend knees deeply

Shift weight toward heels

Reach arms overhead

Engage inner thighs

Draw belly up and in

Surya Namaskara B
Sun Salutation B

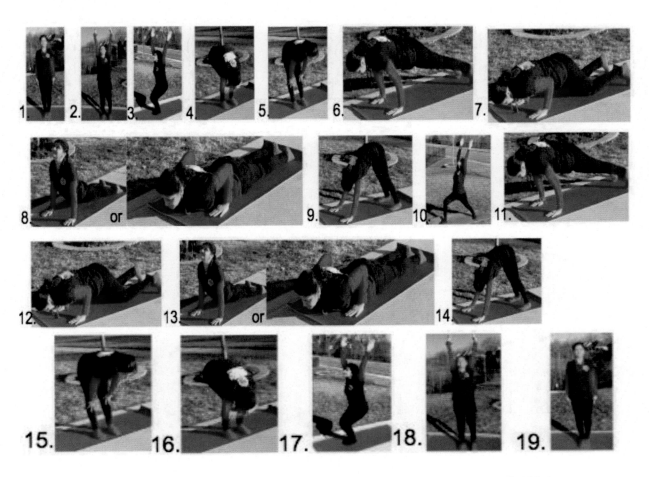

Begin in Tasasana (1.)
Inhale UrdhvaHastasana (2.)
Exhale Utkatasana (3.)
Inhale
Exhale Uttanasana (4.)
Inhale ArdhaUttanasana (5.)
Exhale Phalakasana (6.)
Inhale
Exhale Chaturanga (7.)
Inhale UrdhvaMukhaSvanasana or
Bhujangasana (8.)
Exhale AdhoMukhaSvanasana (9.)

Inhale Virabhadrasana 1 (10.)
Exhale Phalakasana (11.)
Inhale
Exhale Chaturanga (12.)
Inhale UrdhvaMukhaSvanasana or
Bhujangasana (13.)
Exhale AdhoMukhaSvanasana (14.)
*Repeat 10-14 on other side
Step to top of mat
Inhale ArdhaUttanasana (15.)
Exhale Uttanasana (16.)
Inhale Utkatasana (17.)
Exhale Tadasana (18.)

References

Bhagavad Gita

Yoga Sutras of Patanjali

Al Quran (M H Shakir)

The Bible (King James)

Shiva Samhita

Gheranda Samhita

Ved (Ayurved)

Dr Robert O Becker (The Body Electric)

Photos from Google

Compilation Contributed by Xribe .

A Note from the Author

I studied Ayurveda as part of my undergraduate studies. I was impressed by this approach to medicine developed 5000 years ago as all of its teachings and applications concentrate on holistic well-being, which is defined as the balance of mind and body. Ayurveda has been helping people reach a state of balance, so that they can achieve harmony in mind and body in order to gain and maintain optimal health.

My dream is to spread Ayurveda in the United States. Ultimately, I would like to provide Ayurveda as a part of P.E. classes in schools. My vision is to encourage and motivate children and adults alike to live, eat, and follow routines -- the Ayurvedic way.

As a practitioner of Ayurveda, my aim is to help individuals learn how to develop healthier habits and routines day-to-day. Ayurveda is not a system of alternative healing but an ancient science of health and wellness and healing from within. I would like to continue educating, applying and implementing the Ayurvedic approach to help people learn how to reap its benefits. I especially want to educate the younger generation about Ayurveda as it is very important to be able to acquire this knowledge at an early age. I believe this crucial knowledge will help reduce some of the problems that we have recently observed in youth, such as school shootings, excessive indulgence in virtual video games, overuse of "screen time", etc. I believe an important factor involved in the development of these issues is the inability to handle and manage stress and emotions. (Insert a few sentences of how Ayurveda can address stress and emotions in youth).

Fortunately, Ayurvedic principles can be learned and integrated at any stage in life. The benefits are profound for (insert some benefits for adults and describe how Ayurveda can help).

Thus, I also want to continue to teach Ayurveda to adults who may need to enhance their physical and/or emotional well-being, or help individuals manage chronic health issues more effectively. I plan to continue to offer Ayurvedic cooking workshops, educational seminars, and stress management programs. Through this work, I plan to share the benefits Ayurvedic products and approaches and dispel myths about the use of vitamins and minerals, so people can understand how to use such resources most effectively.

Eventually, I would like to open a number of Ayurvedic healing centers throughout the United States so that I can reach out and connect with more people for transforming lives in such a manner that we can pursue health and happiness for the whole of humanity.

About the Author

ArunaPatki B.A.M.S (Director & Founder Ayurveda Healing Spa B.A.M.S., Yoga Teacher, Integrative Healer)

ArunaPatki one of the dedicated Ayurvedic Practitioner & leading experts in Charlotte area of UNITED STATES OF America . She is the only practitioner in the North South East area who practices Authentic Ayurveda For the Healthy way of Living .Her pioneering initiatives in the field of Ayurveda have brought Health, healing, wellness, Happiness in the community of Charlotte and around Charlotte. People travel from NC,SC,TENESSE,VIRGINIA,WV,COLORADO,FLORIDA to seek her guidance in the Detox, health and healing approach. She is a educator in the community who would like to bring a positive change. She has authored and written articles to many magazines in state .With more than 17 years of practice experience, she is one of the few Wholistic PractitionersleadingtheeffortoftrueintegrationofMind-Body-Soulconcept.Sheisaon call practitioner to guide the main stream practitioners the Ayurveda approach for their patients. She studied in Ayurveda at the early age and earned the degree of Bachelor of Ayurvedic Medicine and Surgery (B.A.M.S.), a 5 ½ year program at Ayurvedic. She is Licensed Integrative Bodywork and Massage Therapist, Certified Medical Cupping Therapist is also a active member at several places to spread Ayurveda throughout the USA.

Publications –Charlotte Taste Magazine Natural Awakening Magazine
Radio Show Talk-All Business Media FM Channel ,New York USA 2018

Our Business Information:

Our Website:
http://www.ayurvedahealingspa.com/www.massageayurveda.com/Facebook: ayurvedahealingspa Instagram: ArunaPatki
Contact Us: (704) 808-0708
Therapeutic Retreat, Wellness, and Educational Programs Available.

Name of Business: Ayurveda Healing Spa

Position or Professional Title of the Author: Ayurvedic Practitioner; Founder & President, Ayurveda Healing Spa

Business Location: Concord, Charlotte, NC

Company Background

ArunaPatki is the founder of the Ayurvedic healing center, Ayurveda Healing Spa. She has been serving Ayurveda for the last 16 years. Ayurveda Healing Spa offers authentic Ayurvedic services. By combining Ayurveda, and yoga principles, the Spa has helped thousands shift their lifestyles to bring about balance for complete healing and wellness.

Products/Services Offered at the Ayurvedic Healing Spa

- Ayurvedic Wellness Consultation
- Panchkarma/Detox, Chakra Healing
- Abhyngam (Oil Massage)
- Swedan (Herbal Steam)
- Shirodhara (Third Eye Therapy/Bliss Therapy)
- Udvartana (Exfoliating Massage)
- Herbal Paste Massage
- Gharshan (Massage to Stimulate Blood for Toxin Removal)
- Kati Basti (Oil Pouring on Lower Back)
- Reflexology, Meditation
- Hrud Basti (Pouring of Oil on the Heart Chakra)
- Breathing Techniques(Pranayam)
- Medical Cupping
- Therapeutic Yoga as per Dosha (Body Type Energy)

Education

- BAMS (Bachelor of Ayurvedic Medicine and Surgery), 2001,India
- LMBT#06253 (Licensed Integrative Massage and Body Work Therapist), 2006, USA
- NCBTMB (Nationally Certified Body Work and Massage Therapist),USA
- Yoga Teacher, Practicing for the past 23 years (India, USA), Member of Yoga Alliance2018
- Certified Chakra Healer,USA,
- Certified Medical Cupping Practitioner,USA
- Doctor of Ayurveda (Professional member of NAMAUSA 2019H52447181)

Thank you for contributing in compillation Dr.Elyse , Xribe, Lisa .

I am deeply touched by all my followers who came to seek the help of Ayurved, Yoga, Meditation, Chant, Mantra, Nutrition, Pranayam
(Breathing Techniques) practices.

Thank you God for filling Nector of Ayurved and Yog to heal many more.
Endless Love.

Corporate Therapeutic Yoga, Corporate Wellness Programs, Corporate Stress Management

64786281R00058